T0084290

Connections Are Everything

Connections Are Everything

▼▼▼▼▼▼▼▼▼▼▼▼▼▼▼

A COLLEGE STUDENT'S GUIDE TO

Relationship-Rich Education

▲▲▲▲▲▲▲▲▲▲▲▲▲▲▲

Peter Felten

Leo M. Lambert

Isis Artze-Vega

Oscar R. Miranda Tapia

Johns Hopkins University Press

BALTIMORE

© 2023 Johns Hopkins University Press
All rights reserved. Published 2023
Printed in the United States of America on acid-free paper
2 4 6 8 9 7 5 3

This work is also available in an Open Access edition, which is licensed under a
Creative Commons Attribution– NonCommercial– NoDerivatives 4.0 International
License: https://creativecommons.org/licenses/by-nc-nd/4.0/.C C BY-NC-ND

Johns Hopkins University Press
2715 North Charles Street
Baltimore, Maryland 21218
www.press.jhu.edu

Library of Congress Cataloging-in-Publication

Names: Felten, Peter, author. | Lambert, Leo M., author. | Artze-Vega,
Isis, 1978– author. | Miranda Tapia, Oscar R., 1995– author.
Title: Connections are everything : a college student's guide to
relationship-rich education / Peter Felten, Leo M. Lambert, Isis
Artze-Vega, and Oscar R. Miranda Tapia.
Description: Baltimore : Johns Hopkins University Press, 2023. |
Includes bibliographical references and index.
Identifiers: LCCN 2022057325 | ISBN 9781421443126 (paperback) |
ISBN 9781421445977 (ebook) | ISBN 9781421445960 (ebook other)
Subjects: LCSH: College students—Social networks—United States. |
Communication in higher education—United States. | College
students—United States—Psychology. | Minority college students—
United States. | First-generation college students—United States. |
Nontraditional college students—United States. | Interpersonal
communication. | Interpersonal relations.
Classification: LCC LB3607 .F45 2023 | DDC 378.1/98—dc23/eng/20230221
LC record available at https://lccn.loc.gov/2022057325

A catalog record for this book is available from the British Library.

Special discounts are available for bulk purchases of this book.
For more information, please contact Special Sales at specialsales@jh.edu.

Message of Appreciation

Publication of the free electronic version of this book by Johns Hopkins University Press is made possible by a gift from the John N. Gardner Institute for Excellence in Undergraduate Education (www.jngi.org), dedicated to advancing teaching, learning, student success, equity, and social justice in higher education.

In tribute to the Gardner Institute's Founders—

JOHN N. GARDNER,
Executive Chair of the Board
Distinguished Professor Emeritus, University of South Carolina

BETSY O. BAREFOOT
Senior Scholar

—who have dedicated their careers to student learning and success

Contents

Connections Are Everything

Introduction

Read This First!

WHEN JOSÉ ROBLES signed up for classes his first semester at Nevada State College, he felt like he was stepping into the unknown. No one in his family had ever attended college, and his parents didn't speak English well enough to help him through the process. Still, José describes himself as someone who "just throws myself into things, even if I'm scared." And although José thought he didn't know what he was doing when he enrolled, he knew exactly what he wanted from college: a nursing degree.

That first semester, José was frustrated that he couldn't go right into nursing. He had to take some required classes, including a geology course that didn't interest him and that he wanted to "just get through" as quickly as possible. He didn't know anyone in class on the first day, but he was surprised by the way things unfolded:

> My professor made the course interactive in a way that something as boring as rocks became interesting. The passion she had, she wasn't just giving me information. Her subject was something that she loved. And the way

1

that she explained it, for some reason, I wanted to learn everything about rocks. The most important thing is that the class became a community. She had us interact with each other and with the subject. It just came together because of her passion.

"Something as boring as rocks" changed the way José understood college—and himself. The connections he made with the professor and other students in the class motivated and challenged him to learn, and helped him feel like what he was doing—and who he is—matters. José discovered that a meaningful college experience is relationship rich.

This book is about, and for, students like José. It's for you.

We know how important these kinds of relationships can be. In our careers and personal lives, we have seen many, many students thrive as they connect in college. We've also witnessed too many students struggle and even fail when they don't find what Tianna Guerra, a student at Oakton Community College, calls "that one person who lights a fire within you."

This book will help you find that person—actually, those people—who will transform your college experience.

Who Are We?

The four authors of this book—Isis, Leo, Oscar, and Peter—have accumulated a wide range of experiences in colleges and universities (elsewhere in the book you can find a short biography of each of us). We have worked and studied at community colleges, state universities, small private colleges, big research universities, and the Ivy League. Two of us are first-generation college graduates. We have had a variety of job titles, from president to assistant director, professor to tutor. Beyond higher education, we also have been bartenders, truck drivers, ice cream scoopers, tree nursery workers, and magazine writers. We are from small towns and big cities, we range from millennials to baby boomers, and we grew up in low- to middle-income families. Two of us are bilingual, three of us are parents, one of us is an immigrant, and one is a grandparent. But beyond all these traits, we were also students, and our careers have been dedicated to students just like you.

Why This Book?

We decided to write this book after Leo and Peter published *Relationship-Rich Education* in 2020. That book was written for people who work in higher education. To prepare to write it, Leo and Peter interviewed almost four hundred students, professors, and staff at more than two dozen colleges and universities. One thing they heard repeatedly in those interviews is that students could benefit from knowing more about how important human interactions are in college and how they can make those relationships happen. Leo and Peter discussed that point with Isis and Oscar, and the four of us decided to write a book that aims to do just that.

Throughout this book, we draw on decades of research by higher education scholars. We also build on the interviews Leo and Peter conducted for *Relationship-Rich Education*.

Over the summer of 2021, the four of us interviewed even more students to gather perspectives on how they navigated college during the COVID-19 pandemic, the ongoing racial justice movement, and the contentious election of 2020. Some of the students we interviewed fit the mold of the stereotypical college student—18 to 22 years old, middle class, white, and living on or near their college campus—but many are better described as "new majority" students. This includes students who are commuting or studying fully online, or low income, or parents, or people of color, or queer, or first in their family to go to college, or working full time, or returning to school after time away, or a combination of all of these. Often, new majority students have multiple identities that have been marginalized in or excluded from higher education.

Whether you identify as a "traditional" or "new majority" student (or have parts of both), college is an experience that tends to come with many firsts—your first time going to college, or your first night class or fully online class, or your first time working full time and going to school, or your first time living away from home. Transitions like these can be exciting—and difficult. No matter your identities and situation, you are likely to meet others like you in college.

Why Do Relationships Matter in College?

Popular culture paints a vivid picture of college: friends, parties, sports, romance. Those are important parts of the undergraduate experience for many students, but the vast majority of college students are so busy juggling multiple responsibilities (studying, working, caring for family, and more) that college may not be like what we see on TV, in the movies, or on social media.

When we refer to relationships in college, we're *not* thinking primarily about romantic relationships. Instead, we're focusing on the day-to-day interactions, conversations, and connections you will have with other students and with faculty and staff. Research suggests that your classes, whether in person or online, will probably be the most important place for your relationships to develop. Outside of class, every college and university is also a relationship-rich environment where you will find academic advisors and many other college staff, student clubs and organizations, campus jobs, sports teams, research labs, art studios, music ensembles, and a diverse community of people who can influence your educational journey.

In our interviews, students described many benefits of these kinds of relationships—and what students told us mirrors what's in the research.[1] Positive relationships in college contribute to students' academic success, sense of be-longing, and personal well-being. They do this in part by providing you with a support system of friends, advisors, and mentors who can enhance your college experience in a variety of ways—including academic, emotional, and prac-tical.[2] Students with strong relationships experience more joy and less stress in their daily life. They are more likely to be successful in their classes, as well as professionally after college.[3] They are better able to advocate for themselves and for others. And they learn to see the world, and themselves, from new per-spectives, often discovering new passions and capacities that shape their lives after college.

"There's no right number of friends. There's no right timeline. Just know that you're going to learn so much about yourself through the relationships you form in college."

—Sophie Danish, Davidson College

Yeah, but . . .

Just because relationships are crucial in college doesn't mean it's easy to make or to maintain those connections.

Abraham Segundo knows how hard it can be. After high school in San Antonio, he enrolled at the local community college, "but things really didn't pan out for me." Abraham worked for a few years before he decided he needed to do something different: "When I look around at home, I feel that we deserve better and that some-body needs to spark the change for my nephews and nieces, and for the rest of the family. I decided that I should be the one to do it."

When Abraham returned to college, he carried with him what he had learned at work about the importance of having peers who could help him succeed:

> I feel like too many times students sit there and really struggle because they're too scared to ask for help. I know sometimes my pride gets in the way of asking for help and acknowledging that I don't understand something. My professors are always willing to help me, but it can be intimidating to go to them. For me, as far as a support system, college clubs really have been big. I am part of kinesiology club, and it's a lot of students with the same majors and interests. Those are my people. When school's stressful, I go to the club.

At times, college may be tough, but asking others for help will connect you with folks who will aid you through those challenging moments.

Remember that the responsibility for navigating college does not fall entirely on you. Asking for help is not a sign of weakness; it is a sign of strength and an effective use of your resources. Abraham's new, relational approach to college is helping him be more successful than he would be if he were trying to figure it out on his own. He still struggles with challenging classes plus work and family obligations, but he feels confident knowing that he has people he can count on to reach his goals.

This book will not magically make college difficulties disappear. College can be hard. Relationships in college can be hard. However, we want you to remember two things as you read this book and work your way through college:

1. **You're not alone**. Most students struggle academically and socially at times in college, particularly during their first year. College is a major transition in your life, so periods of struggle are completely normal. Expect them, and know that connecting with peers, faculty, and staff will make college more manageable—and more enjoyable.

2. **You can act** to create for yourself the kind of relationship-rich college experience that will help you reach your goals.

How to Use This Book

This is a different kind of book. While you may choose to read this book from start to finish, you can also jump around and read whatever chapters interest you most. The book is also filled with activities we encourage you to try. You'll see some notes (like the one at the end of this sentence) that will point you to significant research that informs our analysis—and that you might want to read to learn more about a particular topic.[4] If you come across a "college word" you're not familiar with yet, you'll probably find that term in the "College Terms to Know" glossary at the end of the book. You will also notice that we use the words "college" and "university" interchangeably, which is common in the United States but might feel strange if you're not from the US.

Throughout the book you will come across reflection questions, especially in the "Ask Yourself" section near the end of each chapter. We encourage you to ponder these on your own and to talk about them with the people in your life because these are the kinds of questions that benefit from shared thinking. Put simply, "we think *best* when we think *socially*."[5]

You'll also find stories students told us, always with their permission to name and quote them. We are grateful for the perspectives, narratives, and advice they shared. Based on their advice, we outlined small action steps called "Try This!" at the end of each chapter that we hope you will take to begin or continue developing meaningful relationships.

So what's next? This book has nine chapters, divided into three parts. After this introduction, the first three chapters make up a section that focuses on *you*—how you can start by building connections, the common challenges students face in college, and the many strengths you bring with you to college. Part II has three chapters that describe *who you will interact with in college*—the peers, faculty, and staff who will help you transform your learning and life in college. The final part of the book has three chapters that explore *how you can act* through relationship accelerators, mentoring conversations, and constellations of connections to deepen and enrich your college experience. Finally, in the conclusion, "Take These Ideas with You," we offer some big-picture recommendations.

This book is designed to help you build relationships and achieve your aspirations for college. Keep reading, and then commit to taking small but regular steps to connect with your peers, professors, and others in college. You can do this.

PART I

▾▾▼▾▾

Relationships and You

CHAPTER 1

Start with One

WHEN LOGAN THOMAS arrived at North Carolina A&T State University, she had a plan. She had gone to a predominantly white high school in New Jersey, but she applied only to Historically Black Colleges and Universities (HBCUs) where she could study to be an engineer: "Coming to orientation and meeting all these amazing people who look just like me, people who grew up like me, I knew that this is exactly where I want to be." Since Logan had been class president all four years in high school, she intended to be "super involved" at A&T. She immediately began to campaign on social media and in person for election to a leadership role in the Student Government Association.

Then late one night she received an email explaining that she was not eligible to be a candidate because she had not completed all of the necessary steps: "I was so mad at myself. I had one job, and I did not do it." The next morning, she went to see the dean of students: "Me being the annoying and ambitious student that I am, I go up to Dr. Murphy's office. I'm trying to hold my tears in, and I ask her, 'Is there anything that I can do? I am ready for the role, and I want to contribute to A&T.' She listened to me pour out my heart, and then she tells me there are no exceptions." However, Logan's impassioned plea made an impression. Dr. Murphy soon invited her to join the dean's student advisory board: "I went from crying on my couch to gaining a meaningful relationship with Dr. Murphy. And she has been a mentor who has transformed me and opened so many doors for me during my time at A&T."

Logan's experience with Dr. Murphy reveals an important truth about college: One meaningful connection can lead to others. Some students will graduate with a large network of friends and mentors, but research suggests that you don't need a crowd to have a successful college experience:

1. A national poll of 30,000 college graduates found that alumni who reported having **one professor** "who cared about them as a person, made them excited about learning, and encouraged them to pursue their dreams" were more than twice as likely as their peers to be thriving professionally and personally—even many years after graduation.[1]

2. Another national poll showed that graduates who had **a handful of meaningful relationships** with staff and faculty were more than three times as likely as those with no such relationships to say that their time in college was "very rewarding."[2]

In this chapter, we'll tell you a few stories of a connection that acted as the foundation for a student's relationship-rich college experiences. We hope you'll notice how different these initial interactions can be. There is not one path or simple recipe, and some students struggle for a long time to connect with anyone in college. Still, if you are patient and persistent, we are confident you will start to establish the kinds of relationships with peers, faculty, and staff that will contribute to your academic success and personal well-being in college—and some of these people might even become lifelong friends and colleagues.

Start with a Friend

For recent graduate Sydney Stork, who grew up in Iowa, everything started with Wren Renquist, a native of Okinawa, Japan, whom she met during her first semester at the University of Iowa. Wren says Sydney played that role for her too. Sydney knew Wren's first-year roommate because they were in some of the same classes their first semester. Wren's roommate made the introduction, and soon Sydney and Wren began studying together.

The next semester they both took general chemistry, then they each applied to be supplemental instructors (students who help other students learn course material, like learning assistants or peer tutors). Since they were both thinking about careers in medicine, they volunteered together in the same unit of the hospital. "We even started doing undergraduate research at the same time," says Wren. In undergraduate research, students work with a faculty member as a research partner or as part of a faculty member's research team, an opportunity that is important for students considering graduate or professional education like Wren and Sydney. Getting started with undergraduate research can be intimidating, so they helped each other feel confident enough to try. Wren describes their relationship as a mirror: "I think everything that Sydney did, I did, and everything I did, Sydney did."

What did it mean to them to have each other as friends starting in that first year? Thinking back shortly after she graduated, Sydney describes Wren as "probably the most constant thing throughout my college career." The adjective "constant" may not seem like a big deal, but college is a time of a lot of change, so it helps to have something or someone steady in your life. As Sydney puts it, "We've both changed our minds about everything we started out here doing, but despite that, we've carried each other through and supported each other through all the ups and downs."

Start with a Professor

Tianna Guerra, a student at Oakton Community College and an aspiring orthopedic surgeon, remembers that when she got to college, she was placed into the lowest-level math class. She was disappointed because she had a lot of courses to complete to stay on track toward her academic goals. What she did not know was that her interactions with her math professor, Mario Borha, would inspire her through college. Tianna told us, "He really started me off on the path of realizing that few are born geniuses and that if you want to learn and become great, it is through hard work, support, and dedication." With his help and encouragement, she finished two math classes in one semester and later became president of the math club, where she made many new friends and connected with other professors, all while gaining valuable leadership experience. Professor Borha served as a key catalyst for Tianna's relationships—and success—in college.

Start with a Member of the College Staff

A native of Afghanistan, Meena Alizai had been in the United States for only a few years when she realized she had a choice: she could stay forever in her current job at the Dollar Store, or she could work toward her academic dreams for herself and her two small children. She made the decision to go to college to become a nurse. Even though she had a goal, at first Meena felt lost. Her courses at San Antonio College's Center for English Language Learning were challenging, and everything about being a student in the US was new to her. One day Meena learned from a classmate that the Empowerment Center was giving away diapers to help students who were parents, and she went to get some for her baby. Meena had never visited the center on campus, but she had heard that it provided a wide range of academic, social, and economic support and resources for students at the college.

When Meena stopped by to pick up some diapers, she met Bertha Castellanos, an advisor who works at the center. Bertha asked Meena what she was studying, and soon they were talking about Meena's academic goals and the family, work, and school obligations she juggled every day. Just like that, everything changed. Bertha helped Meena apply for scholarships to pay for her tuition and cover daycare costs, guided her in putting together her course schedule each semester, and offered her advice about studying effectively. Some semesters, they would talk every week. In Meena's words, "If I didn't meet Bertha, college wouldn't be possible for me, because she really helped me during everything." Meena has since completed her English as a Second Language program and an associate in science degree; she is now a nursing student who has a small but growing network of friends and mentors at San Antonio College.

What If You Haven't Connected with Someone Yet?

Despite these stories, you might still be worried if a semester or more has passed and you have not yet found someone with whom you meaningfully connect. Or you might have transferred to a different institution so even though you're not new to college, you're new at your school. Or you might be so busy with work, family obligations, and other things that you just haven't had the time or energy to build relationships. You're not alone. In fact, lots of students are in the same situation.

When we talked to University of Iowa student Samer Suleman, he told us that during his first two years of college, he was doing well academically but "was hopping around from place to place" and "spent a lot of time honestly feeling isolated socially." Although he remained close with some friends from high school, he didn't feel much hope of connecting with peers or professors at the university. That changed when he found the Multicultural and International Student Support and Engagement (MISSE) program during his junior year: "I've been at MISSE for less than a year, and it has been pretty transformative in terms of the relationships I've been able to build as well as just the ways I feel supported. Everyone there takes time to get to know you, and then they sponsor and invite you to try new things and connect with new people."

Samer's story is far more common than you might think. In fact, when they met, Sydney did not know Wren would become her best friend. Tianna did not expect to connect with her math professor. And Meena went to the Empowerment Center to pick up diapers, not to find a mentor. The opportunities for these kinds of human connections in college are all around you, if you start looking for them. You may be surprised to find out just how many

FACT: **Non-teaching staff are everywhere.** In fall 2019, more than 2.5 million individuals in *non-teaching* positions worked in US colleges and universities.* Whether they are advisors or counselors, serve as tutors, support student clubs, work in an academic department, keep technology running smoothly, or do something else altogether, the point is that *your* Bertha Castellanos can be anywhere at your college or university.

*National Center for Education Statistics, Institute of Education Sciences, US Department of Education, "Employees and Instructional Staff: How Many People Are Employed by Postsecondary Institutions?" accessed November 30, 2021, https://nces.ed.gov/ipeds/TrendGenerator/app/answer/5/30.

people work at your college or university in offices that exist to support students like you.

When we asked Abraham Segundo, from San Antonio College, what advice he would give to his peers, he stressed the importance of these resources: "Take advantage of all the opportunities available on campus; there's plenty of different resources. If you have mental health concerns, or if you need counseling services, or if you're not food secure, there's plenty of different college resources that students often don't know about." And each of these resources is coordinated by professionals who are there to support and connect with you. One of them could absolutely become a catalyst for relationships in college for you.

Connections All around You

If you think about it, every student in every class is potentially a meaningful connection for you. And you already have something in common to talk about with them: the class. Getting together to study is a good idea for many reasons (as discussed in chapter 4). Among other things, it will give you an "accountability buddy," making it more likely that you will actually set aside time to study. You'll also have someone to explain things to and to test you, both of which are excellent study strategies.[3]

But connecting to another student does not have to begin with studying. When Olegaria Gonzalez was admitted to Nevada State College, she looked up the school on Instagram. She soon discovered clubs and events that interested her, and she started following students, staff, and faculty who shared her interests. Before she even went to her first class, she had begun to build the foundation for relationships she would develop in person: "Instagram helped me a lot to connect with people at Nevada State. At first, I mostly learned about what was happening and who was involved already."

FACT: **Social media can help.** Instagram and other apps can be powerful tools for making connections. Social media can be especially helpful in forming relationships if you attend college mostly or fully online. Some of the potential downsides of social media are probably familiar to you, including the way it tends to portray "perfect" (or at least misleading and incomplete) versions of life that can leave people feeling inadequate and lonely.[1] And many college students—like other people—tend to believe that everyone else has more friends than they do, even though that's not usually the case.[2]

But social media can help you establish personal connections and maintain existing friendships as you transition in and through college, which can make the challenges of higher education easier to navigate.[3] The key is to use social media intentionally in ways that support your learning and well-being. For example, social media can be good for creating initial or informal connections between you and new peers, or with staff and faculty at your institution; to make the most of your time in college, you can then take deliberate steps to build stronger relationships with a few of those people, knowing that some of them might become important friends and mentors.[4]

---

[1]Matthew Pittman and Brandon Reich, "Social Media and Loneliness: Why an Instagram Picture May Be Worth More Than a Thousand Twitter Words," *Computers in Human Behavior* 62 (September 1, 2016): 155–67, https://doi.org/10.1016/j.chb.2016.03.084.

[2]Scott L. Feld, "Why Your Friends Have More Friends Than You Do," *American Journal of Sociology* 96, no. 6 (May 1, 1991): 1464–77, https://doi.org/10.1086/229693.

[3]David C. DeAndrea et al., "Serious Social Media: On the Use of Social Media for Improving Students' Adjustment to College," in "Social Media in Higher Education," special issue, *The Internet and Higher Education* 15, no. 1 (January 1, 2012): 15–23, https://doi.org/10.1016/j.iheduc.2011.05.009.

[4]Sherry Turkle, *Alone Together: Why We Expect More from Technology and Less from Each Other* (New York: Basic Books, 2017).

You don't need dozens (or tens of thousands) of connections to be successful in college. *One* meaningful relationship can serve as a catalyst for meeting new people and developing the skills and confidence you need to get on the path to a relationship-rich college experience. The intentional steps you take to cultivate meaningful connections will help you thrive academically and personally in college.

That's easier said than done, so the next chapter will explore some of the common challenges students face with making human connections in college.

 ## Ask Yourself . . .

1. Have you met anyone yet who might be the "start" to your relationship-rich education? If you have, how will you deepen this relationship?

2. If you haven't found that person yet, make a list of people who could potentially be an initial connection for you. If you don't have specific people in mind, you might just list categories of people (for example, a professor, or a student who has already been admitted to the nursing program). How can you begin to establish connections with this person or these people?

3. Could you help someone else start their relationship building? What could you do to help that person make meaningful connections in college?

 ## Try This!

1. Follow your college on social media to find out about upcoming events. Choose one to attend, whether in person or virtually, then hang around for a few minutes after it ends to chat with people there about the event.

2. Find out where the career services staff are located or how to access online assistance (by searching on your college

website), and make an appointment to talk to someone about your career goals.

3. Get to one of your classes early, look for a friendly face, and introduce yourself. A simple, "Hi, I'm ___; it's nice to meet you" can be enough for an initial connection.

CHAPTER 2

College Comes with Challenges

SYDNEY STORK from the University of Iowa, whom you met in chapter 1, told us that in college "everyone's going through something scary and new":

> For some students, this may be the first time being on their own, away from their parents. Maybe they're in a different state or a different country than where they grew up. Maybe they're experiencing a totally different culture. Or maybe they're uncertain about what they want to do with their life, and they're having to make all these big decisions right now.

Like Sydney, you may be asking yourself some big questions. Am I smart enough? How will I balance my studies, my job, and my family responsibilities? What if my roommate is weird? How will I pay for college? How will I meet people if I'm taking classes only online?

Whatever you may be concerned about, remember that it's common to be anxious about college, especially during the first few weeks of an academic year. This is true for almost every student,

FACT: **It can be harder to connect online.** Research shows that the physical separation that comes with online learning can make it more difficult to form and maintain connections. As a result, online students are more likely to feel a sense of isolation.* If your life permits, take one or more in-person classes, especially during your first year of college. Otherwise, use opportunities like class discussions and virtual office hours to connect with your peers and professors. Also explore clubs and organizations that meet online and virtual events hosted by your college.

*Janine Delahunty, Irina Verenikina, and Pauline Jones, "Socio-emotional Connections: Identity, Belonging, and Learning in Online Interactions: A Literature Review," *Technology, Pedagogy, and Education* 23, no. 2 (2014): 243–265.

and doubly so if you are a transfer student or if you are facing serious life challenges outside of college.[1] Developing strong coping skills and a personal support system will help you manage the many transitions you go through in college and will help you reach your goals for the future.[2] As Sydney so aptly stated, a key step in navigating college is to "surround yourself with *people*."

In this chapter, we will illuminate some of the obstacles you may encounter while in college or concerns you already have about connecting with others. We will feature stories of students navigating these challenges. Our hope is to help you identify common difficulties for students and to equip you with strategies to create a college experience that is filled with meaningful relationships that will enable to you thrive academically and personally.

Concerns about Peers

Moon Medina grew up in north Florida, just 10 minutes from the Georgia border. After moving hundreds of miles to attend Florida International University (FIU), Moon said, "I had to completely start over when I moved to Miami. I had no friends in the city whatso-ever." Kayla Neal did not have to go nearly so far from home to attend the University of Michigan–Flint, but they still wondered, "Who's going to be my best friend while I'm in college?" Kayla also worried about joining a student organization on campus: "Everyone there probably knows each other already; they're probably really cliquey."

As a first-year student at the University of Iowa, Alexa Oleson had a plan for dealing with peers: avoid them. "I was super shy when I first came to campus," said Alexa. "I was really bad at talking to people, especially strangers. I would just freeze up. When I would go to class, I would sit down and look as unwelcoming as possible. I did not want anyone to sit next to me." A professor noticed this about Alexa and encouraged her to get a job at the Conversation Center, which provides opportunities for international students to practice conversations in English with trained peer consultants. After going through the training, Alexa still felt unsure:

> In my very first Conversation Center appointment, I went in and was so nervous I was shaking. I felt I had a panic attack coming on. I was sitting and this other student walks up and sits across from me, and he looks ten times as nervous as I do. He literally has sweat beading on his forehead, and he just looked so nervous. But his anxiety kind of helped me calm down because I realized that we were both in the same position where we were so afraid to talk to each other. So, you just calm down and ground yourself. It's just a conversation.

Even for student leaders, interacting with peers might not be as easy as it looks. Jennyflore Andre is a learning assistant, a peer educator responsible for facilitating interactions among students in the classroom, at FIU. The goal is to have students actively sharing ideas with one another and learning together. Before college, Jennyflore had years of experience working with children, but engaging with her peers seemed different: "At first, it was scary. I have always been a shy student. I am better at interacting with little kids than my own college classmates." However, Jennyflore soon became comfortable and skilled at helping her peers connect with each other and with the course content.

Oftentimes small steps—like saying "hi" to a classmate on the first day of class, responding positively to a peer's post on an online discussion board, inviting someone to have coffee after class, joining a pick-up basketball game, sending an email to a professor, introducing yourself to a staff member in the career center—can spark meaningful connections. Kayla soon discovered that college does not need to be as difficult as some make it seem: "It's so refreshing knowing that college is different. It's so much better than high school, because the people here actually care about you and what you are doing. They want to help you learn." Moon ended up making many friends they are still in touch with today. And Jennyflore became so effective as a learning assistant to her peers that she was asked to take on a leadership role in the program.

Concerns about Professors and Staff

David Latimer, an advisor to hundreds of students at City Tech, part of the City University of New York, told us that in thousands of hours of conversations with students over the years he has heard a common theme:

> Students fear failure and being challenged beyond their
> limits. They may not have been challenged academically
> in high school, and for the first time are really experiencing
> academic rigor. They fear embarrassing their families—

being afraid to come home and say, "I am not achieving in college right now. I'm struggling." They fear talking to a professor because a professor represents an intimidating authority figure. They are not sure how to approach them. They also resist asking for help or asking for a tutor, because utilizing a tutor is perceived as not being smart. They do not want to go to counseling when they have emotional concerns, because that's for people who are weak. The fear of shame is everywhere.

Latimer repeats the word "fear" several times, pointing out that it often gets in the way of student success. He has made a critical difference in the lives of hundreds of CUNY students because he spends time with his advisees and gets to know their stories and hopes and dreams, and he helps them overcome their fears. You will find many David Latimers on your campus—people who want to get to know you and be part of your support system, but you also have to do your part to establish a connection. This usually involves taking a small first step, like sending an email to schedule an advising conversation.

Sometimes an initial contact with a professor or staff member might go less well than expected. Sam Owusu, a graduate of Davidson College with a degree in international relations, told a

☑ **FACT:** **Negativity happens.** Negative interactions and occasional loneliness can be a part of everyday life.* Sometimes people are rude or dismissive. These moments can sting, but try not to allow another person's negativity push you off of your path toward thriving. Talking with a friend or a counselor at your college can help you gain perspective.

*Sherry Turkle, *Alone Together: Why We Expect More from Technology and Less from Each Other* (New York: Basic Books, 2017).

story about saying something to his professor on the first day of class that could be perceived as rude, although that was not his intent. Sam recalls, "I felt so bad because I thought the relationship was over. I had just insulted this person. But after class, I went up and apologized to her, and she said she appreciated that." This same faculty member eventually ended up being Sam's major advisor and one of his most important mentors. Awkward moments in college like Sam's are not uncommon, but if you respond with courtesy and respect, you will usually find that most people will be forgiving and remain open to a positive relationship with you.

Imposter Syndrome

Fear and anxiety are serious barriers to a relationship-rich college experience and are related to "imposterism" or "imposter syndrome." It is common for students—and for all people—to sometimes doubt whether they have what it takes to be successful and to fit into new, challenging environments.[3] Experiences in college may magnify these doubts, causing students to feel like "imposters" who are only pretending to belong in college. In many ways this is a normal part of adjusting to college. Gigi Gaultier, a student at the University of Washington, told us about her first days on campus: "Sitting in these large classrooms—Chemistry 142 had 500 people or so—I convinced myself that they're all more successful than me. I was comparing myself to others and imagining all of their accomplishments. I was freaking out."

One way some students try to manage these feelings is do what George Mason University sociology professor Blake Silver calls retreating into superficial cookie-cutter versions of themselves.[4] To try to fit in, these students act like stereotypes, often connected to their gender or race. Young women might play the role of "the mom of the group," and athletes might pose like "the cool guys." Although it may be tempting or seem easier to play a familiar role, that behavior actually reinforces your sense of imposterism and does not establish the authentic connections with peers that can help you begin to feel you belong in college.

The hidden codes and customs of college can make imposterism even worse. Faculty and staff often use terms that they understand but that can be confusing to people who are new to higher education: "syllabus," "prerequisite," "office hours," "department chair," and more (see this book's glossary, "College Terms to Know," for definitions). And students often have habits of studying, reading, writing, and thinking that do not always serve them well in the face of the rigors of college courses, so even students who were successful in high school cannot necessarily rely on what has worked for them in the past.[5] The experience of being academically unsuccessful on an assignment or exam (particularly if you're used to earning high grades) adds to a feeling of not being as prepared as everyone else.

When we met Joshua Rodriguez, a 30-year-old first-generation student at Oakton Community College, near Chicago, he talked to us about one of his classes:

Early in my Calculus 2 class, Professor Arco started getting into really difficult things, and I suddenly began having these feelings like I didn't belong in this class—that my education, what I was trying to achieve, wasn't possible, and my goals were just obscenely farther away than I thought they were. I fell a little behind on homework and went to Professor Arco to say that I might have to drop out. He told me, "Joshua, I want you to go home, and I don't want you to do the homework tonight. What I want you to do is, I want you to look up imposter syndrome and read about it. Then, right before our next class, come and talk to me." I did that, and I learned that it is extraordinarily common among students. That interaction bolstered my confidence to realize that I am not alone in this, that everyone has these feelings. And I went from contemplating dropping out and not pursuing my degree to going and getting tutoring help, which is free here at Oakton. I ended up getting an A in the class, and it was entirely because of that one simple interaction. One conversation with Professor Arco was the difference between me not being a student anymore and me being a successful student achieving a 4.0.

Fortunately, Joshua was able to build up the courage to speak with Professor Arco. This conversation empowered him to bounce back from this difficult moment. More important, that one critical interaction led Joshua to persist in community college and then go on to transfer to (and eventually graduate from) the nuclear engineering program at Purdue University.

While feelings of imposter syndrome are common among all college students, students with historically marginalized identities in higher education may feel more pressure and more like imposters than their peers. Being the only student of color in your classroom, not seeing professors or college leaders who look like you, not feeling like you have financial access to academic or social opportunities, or reading textbooks that make no mention of your culture can make you feel like you do not belong. Social inequities also powerfully shape students' time in college. Khadijah Seay, a student at Bryn Mawr College, told us: "Coming to college was a difficult experience for me. There was the just being away from home part. And then there was race. I never felt like I was a student first. I was always Black first, then a student." Khadijah's experience is all too common. Students who carry traditionally marginalized

☑ **FACT:** Some college students find it difficult to extend trust. Trust has been called the glue that binds educational relationships together,[1] but a study of college students found that Black, Latinx, multiracial, and other groups of students had lower levels of trust than white students.[2] There are many understandable reasons for mistrust, but we encourage you to give others the benefit of the doubt and not let it get in the way of your relationship building.

[1]Stephen Brookfield, *The Skillful Teacher: On Technique, Trust, and Responsiveness in the Classroom* (John Wiley & Sons, 1990).

[2]Kevin Fosnacht and Shannon Calderone, "Who Do Students Trust? An Exploratory Analysis of Undergraduates' Social Trust" (presentation, 45th Annual Conference of the Association for the Study of Higher Education, New Orleans and virtual, November 20, 2020).

identities often struggle to develop a sense of belonging in college.[6] That can make academic and social success more difficult to achieve, even though these same students also bring significant assets and capacities to college with them (more on this in chapter 3).

We cannot emphasize enough how valuable it is for students of color like Khadijah to find campus offices, services, and student organizations that have been created to support Black, Latinx, Native, Asian and Pacific Islander, and other student identities.[7] These offices are led by professional staff who have become transformative mentors in the lives of many students. If your college doesn't have one of these offices or you can't find the time to connect to one of them, focus on making meaningful connections with other students, professors, and college employees (see the chapters in part II for ideas). Research tells us that what's most important for students of color and those from other socially oppressed identity groups (including individuals with disabilities and members of the LGBTQ community) is to form deep relationships in which they feel comfortable being themselves.[8] With these deeper relationships in place, students know they truly belong. That might mean pausing to ask yourself, as you meet people, "Am I pretending to be something I'm not, or can I be myself?" And then spend more time with those who recognize your awesomeness.

What to Do?

Almost every student entering college faces unfamiliarity with new environments, people, and terminology, and most sometimes feel socially isolated and have at least a bit of imposter syndrome. You should recognize how completely *common* it is to have these experiences in college. You are not alone, and in fact your struggles are shared by the overwhelming majority of your peers.

Some students also will experience major stressors, like anxiety that feels overwhelming or unmanageable, physical health concerns, loss of a loved one, or hunger and homelessness. If that is true for you, do not delay—contact your college's health service, counseling center, disability resources service, and the array of other support services that are there for you. This kind of help-seeking behavior is essential for your well-being and your academic success. Too often, students don't think these resources are available to them, or they feel embarrassed to ask for help.[9]

One student told us that she finally came to the realization that "it was not cheating to use college resources" like the tutoring and counseling centers. Indeed, not only are these services vital to your success, but they are staffed by caring people who could become some of the most encouraging mentors you will find in college. In our experience, the sooner college resources are a part of your support system, the sooner you will feel connected to your community, and you will be on the path to academic and personal well-being.

The challenges of college can feel overwhelming. Remember that a great many people at your college want you to succeed and

TABLE 2.1. Key College Resources for Navigating Life Challenge

LIFE CHALLENGES	COLLEGE RESOURCES
Anxiety, depression, mental health concerns	College counseling center Health services Disability resources
Physical health and medication management	Health services
Learning differences	Disability resources
Hunger and homelessness	Financial aid Institutional emergency funds College food pantry Chaplain's office
Citizenship and visa concerns	International student and scholar services, offices that serve DACA students

Note: DACA, which stands for Deferred Action for Childhood Arrivals, is a policy that protects young people—known as DREAMers—who were brought to the United States without documentation as children.

will do what they can to help you flourish. To connect with those people and resources, we have two main pieces of advice:

1. **Don't do college alone.** College can be lonely, but you are surrounded by faculty, staff, and peers who can support you. Connect with the people and programs at your college, and don't wait until there's a crisis to begin establishing relationships. Visit the writing center early in the semester to get feedback on a draft paper; check out the tutoring center to see how it works before your first big test is looming. And draw on the many resources at your college (see table 2.1 for examples of key resources your school is likely to offer).

2. **Take the initiative to connect.** You will be very busy in college, but make time to intentionally reach out to establish

relationships. The students profiled in this chapter faced many challenges, and they summoned the courage to take one brave step to connect with someone. You can

- reach out to a professor or staff member you think you might like to get to know better
- join a club or organization where you sense a special affiliation
- talk to the person sitting next to you in class or in your online breakout room
- share your feelings of imposterism with someone you trust
- visit an office that provides academic support to students, such as academic advising
- make an appointment to talk with a professional in the counseling center or through a virtual counseling service your college may offer

A few small steps can be pivotal for you. As you build relationships, you will begin to feel less alone, and you will have people who can support and challenge you through the ups and downs of college.

In the next chapter, we are going to focus on the strengths, skills, and personal qualities you already possess to navigate college. Be confident that you have an array of talents that you will draw on to lead you toward success.

 **Ask Yourself . . .**

1. What is the most significant challenge you are feeling about making the transition into or your time in college?

2. What is one simple, concrete action you could take as a positive step to address this challenge?

3. Who is one person at your college (a professor, staff member, or peer) who might help you address this challenge? How can you connect with that person?

 ## Try This!

1. Join one or two student clubs or organizations (in person or online) where you think you might "find your people." It's usually better to focus on a small number of clubs or organizations where you can really get involved rather than over-committing to too many groups and making shallower connections.

2. Make it a habit to introduce yourself to peers you meet in class or on campus. Simply learning the names of other people is often the first step in building relationships.

3. Not every college student has concerns about building new relationships with peers. If that describes you, consider taking on a peer leadership role early in your time in college because your interpersonal skills and confidence can help others make connections and find their way.

4. If you have any concerns pertaining to physical or mental health, if you have a learning difference, or if you would like to use another college resource necessary for your success, find the appropriate office (online or on campus) and email or stop by to set up an initial conversation with someone who can help you understand what is available to you as a student.

CHAPTER 3

You Have What It Takes

IN CHAPTER 2 you met Gigi Gaultier, a student at the University of Washington who says she spent much of her first year "comparing myself to others and imagining all of their accomplishments. I was freaking out about a lot of things at first." As we described, Gigi's doubts—her sense of being an imposter—are shared by many, many college students. A student we interviewed at a selective liberal arts college described being "mortified by my own seeming deficits and by feeling paralyzed by comparison and insecurity." A very accomplished community college student introduced herself to us by saying, "I come from an academically challenged background. I wasn't the best student in high school, so I just assumed I wasn't smart enough for college." Those feelings are real, yet they do not tell the whole story.

We began this part of the book by showing you that you can start your relationship-rich education by connecting to just one person. In this chapter we emphasize that *you* are the key actor in forming these relationships and creating a meaningful college experience. No matter where you attend, your school has lots of resources and people to support and challenge you—so it's not *all* on you. The faculty and staff at your college should, and likely will, do a lot to enable your success, and other students also can be your allies, friends, and champions. But it all begins with you, and, as this chapter describes, you bring many strengths to college that will help you form meaningful relationships and reach your goals. Change can be exciting and uncomfortable, but if you choose to act and to raise your voice, you will find that you have what it takes to thrive.

Recognize the Many Strengths You Bring to College

Donna Linderman leads the Accelerated Study in Associate Programs (known as ASAP), which helps thousands of students succeed every year at the City University of New York. The students in this program typically work while they attend school, and most are the first in their family to go to college. She told us:

Many of our students haven't necessarily tapped into the gifts and the skills they already have—their own tenacity, their own intelligence. We help them understand that they are fully capable—every single one of them—of earning their degrees. We ask, "What are the things that you've worked toward and achieved?" Whether it's being a great parent, being a productive member of your family, enjoying some subject in school that really resonated with you, or something else that helps them identify the strengths in themselves.

This program is transformational, partly because ASAP's advisors and faculty help students recognize and draw on the strengths they bring with them to college.

Sometimes those strengths are obvious, like when a student developed strong math skills in high school or has a part-time job writing a blog for a local news station. More often, however, students don't fully see the strengths they bring to school. Some of you might have trouble seeing yours. Tara Yosso, a professor of education at the University of California, Riverside, has written about these powerful but often unrecognized strengths.[1] A student who grew up speaking a language other than English might feel hesitant about writing and speaking in a college classroom, not noticing the sophisticated thinking and communication skills they have developed as they navigate the world in more than one language; Yosso calls this "linguistic capital." And a student who has struggled against social inequities or personal tragedies in their life brings to college an "aspirational capital" that helps them maintain hope and persist in the face of great difficulties.

In a similar way, a student who works full time or is a parent will have to juggle many pressing responsibilities yet may not recognize that they bring to college the ability to manage time and prioritize what's most important. Students who have experiences as athletes, musicians, artists, and gamers know the value of practicing, learning from mistakes, and continuing to work through the most challenging times—all essential to college success. Many students know someone who believes in them more than they believe in themselves, and that person's encouragement can give them the extra boost of energy and commitment necessary when things get hard.

We are *not* saying that being a student is easy or the same for everybody. Of course, it's not. Instead, we encourage you to spend some time noticing your strengths that will help you succeed in

▼▼▼▼▼▼▼▼▼▼▼▼▼▼▼▼

"Another strategy that I have: telling myself when I wake up in the morning that I can do anything. Tell myself: if I put my mind to it, I can achieve it."

—Brandon Daye, North Carolina A&T State University

▲▲▲▲▲▲▲▲▲▲▲▲▲▲▲▲▲▲

college. As Donna Linderman told us, that is essential for you to be able to say and believe, "I am good at things, I can commit to things, and I can finish them."

You don't need to do this on your own. In fact, talking with peers or an advisor can be a particularly effective way to recognize the strengths you have. Asma Shauib credits her professors at LaGuardia Community College with helping her see through her struggles as a first-generation, immigrant, working, and multilingual student to recognize the personal assets that would help her succeed:

> The faculty believed in me more than I did in myself. They asked me to share my thoughts and my ideas, my goals, my dreams of what I wanted to be, what I wanted to achieve. I did that, but deep inside me, I did not think that any of that was possible, especially for someone from my background and culture. But they told me that those are great ideas and we can see you achieving them. When they first said that to me, I thought, "No one has ever told me that." They see that in me, and I keep that in mind whenever I'm stressed out or think that I will not make it.

In the same way, Davidson College student Sam Owusu's academic advisor made a big difference for him: "She really pushed me to have some faith in myself." Having a little faith in yourself is foundational. When you weave together your personal strengths with the resources at your college (peers, faculty, staff, and student support programs), you will be even more likely to meet your goals.[2]

Many of the examples of strengths just described are abilities, attitudes (like confidence), or kinds of knowledge, but you have even more sources of strength: your existing relationships and the people in your life. For instance, University of Michigan–Flint student Amena Shukairy, who lived at home during her college

FACT: **Family can be a source of strength.** A study examining social support among first-generation and non-first-generation students found that a significant number of students identified parents as extremely important forms of emotional support throughout their time in college.[1] Professor Tara Yosso describes this source of capital as familial capital.[2]

[1] L. Nichols and Á. Islas, "Pushing and Pulling Emerging Adults through College: College Generational Status and the Influence of Parents and Others in the First Year," *Journal of Adolescent Research* 31, no. 1 (2016): 59–95, https://doi.org/10.1177/0743558415586255.

[2] Tara J. Yosso, "Whose Culture Has Capital? A Critical Race Theory Discussion of Community Cultural Wealth," *Race Ethnicity and Education* 8, no. 1 (March 1, 2005): 69–91, https://doi.org/10.1080/1361332052000341006.

years, told us, "My family members are, hands down, my number-one supporters." Your closest friends, whether or not they attend your college or any college, can also be assets. They might provide you with emotional support, help you unwind, or remind you of your values or motivations for earning a degree. You might find other assets in your social media networks. Recent DePaul University graduate Brian Chan told us, "I use LinkedIn, and a common piece of advice that I was always given is just reach out to as many people as possible. And eventually, there'll be someone who will have a similar situation to you or can relate to that level or know someone who they can introduce you to." Although social media connections are sometimes superficial, each connection has the potential to evolve into a lasting relationship if you devote time to it.

Recognize That Change Is Exciting *and* Uncomfortable

Once you've started to think carefully and creatively about who you are—and about the strengths you bring to college—the next step is to consider who you are becoming. College, after all, is a time when you should learn, grow, and change.

Ruth Moreno worked for more than a decade after high school before deciding to continue her education. At first, she "felt like a dinosaur" sitting in class with many younger students at San Antonio College. When her advisor encouraged her to apply for the Honors Academy, "that seemed like a joke to me" because she didn't see herself as an honors student: "I was scared of having more rigorous classes and then not being able to make As in those classes." Her advisor's persistence, however, convinced Ruth to get outside of her comfort zone.

The process was not simple. First Ruth had to really listen to what her advisor said and convince herself to act. After she applied and was accepted to the Honors Academy, she had to commit to new classes, new professors, new peers, and new academic work. That felt scary. Reflecting back, however, Ruth smiled as she described thriving in the Honors Academy, which set her up to earn an undergraduate degree with honors and to pursue a master's degree in business.

Samantha Paskvan also had to stretch herself further than she expected in college. When she left home in Alaska to attend the University of Washington, she planned to major in chemistry. After taking a few chemistry courses, she did not feel that spark of excitement that she had anticipated, and she began to wonder if she should pursue her passion for dance instead. To her surprise, a genetics course changed her mind. She found herself enjoying the professor, the course content, and the peer conversations in this active learning class. After the class ended, Samantha approached her professor to ask about the possibility of doing undergraduate research. Once she joined a professor's genetics lab, Samantha discovered she loved both using her "science brain" and being in a scientific community doing meaningful work together:

Beyond the serious science we're doing, there's this whole other aspect of caring about each other's lives. The faculty will make the time to ask, How are your classes going? What are you thinking about for next year? What are you getting involved in outside of the lab? Who do you want to be after you graduate? And then they would really listen and encourage me, even when I wasn't sure if I knew what I was doing or where I was going.

Samantha continued to pursue her interest in genetics after graduation, going to work in a research lab that uses genomic science to develop new ways to prevent and treat cancer. Her path to that lab wasn't always smooth, but Samantha persisted and acted when she identified a new passion she wanted to pursue.

You Have Agency

You may be asking yourself, well, where do I start? My college offers so many programs, events, and activities. How do I choose what to do and who to connect with? As a student, you have what some call "agency"—the ability to make choices and to take actions that matter. How you choose to use that agency will have a profound influence on your college experiences. In fact, scholars who study higher education have found that "what students *do* in college is far more important than the type of institution they attend."[3]

Don't just drift through college aimlessly.[4] Like Samantha Paskvan, whom you met earlier this chapter, your agency allows you to act on your intellectual curiosity and passions. If things aren't going so well, you can use your agency to contact one of your professors when something seems unfair or is getting in the way of your learning. And if that doesn't work, you have the agency to reach out to a department chair or dean to express your concerns.

If you have flexibility in your schedule (like elective courses in your college's core curriculum), you can choose to take a class that interests you but is not connected to your career goals. Join a student club to pursue one of your passions or to try something completely new (like student dance clubs that welcome novices and that can be a great way to have fun and learn about another culture). Go to a musical performance, a play, or an art exhibit offered by other students to see what your peers can do. Contact a few classmates on social media to see if they will form an online study group as you prepare for a big exam or will join forces with you to reach out to college leaders with a suggestion that will help your fellow students. Throughout the book, you'll read about how students like you used their agency to connect with people, learn new things, and follow their dreams. What you do with your agency is up to you!

In the first couple of chapters, we introduced you to students who struggled to connect because they felt too shy or too busy or too independent or too old or too different or too academically unsure. Not all students are like that. Dylan Costo decided not to waste a minute of his time at Florida International University. In his first semester, Dylan was so interested in a particular topic in physics that he looked up the research interests of faculty in the physics department and then knocked on the office door of Professor Jorge Rodriguez: "He looked up and said, 'Hi, who are you?' I told him, 'I'm not a student in your class, but I want to talk about your research.' And that short interaction led to a four-year conversation. I still drop by his office regularly to talk about physics." All it took was a quick search on the university website and then the courage to knock on Professor Rodriguez's door.

Even if you're not as bold as Dylan, you still have the capacity to start making meaningful connections with students, faculty, and peers in college. The next section of the book will dig more deeply into why these relationships matter and how you can make them happen.

 # Ask Yourself . . .

1. Looking back on your life, what are the things you've worked toward and achieved? What did you do (for example, practice every day or ask questions of someone who knows more than you) and what did you believe (for example, "I can do this" and "I won't give up") that made it possible for you to achieve those things? How can you apply those same practices and beliefs to your college experience?

2. If we asked the people who know you best (for instance, your closest friends, family, spouse, kids, or colleagues) to describe your strengths, what would they tell us?

3. Take a moment to reflect on where you want to be after college. What do you imagine yourself doing? With whom may you want to connect or continue being connected with along this journey?

 # Try This!

1. Take a few minutes to list your strengths in each of the six categories below, and then think about how your different strengths could help you succeed and thrive in college:[5]

- social (for example, ability to relate to others, ability to maintain relationships for a long time)
- academic (ability in writing, math, computing, or another subject area)
- athletic (skill at a team or individual sport)
- artistic (skill in drawing, singing, music, or other creative pursuits)
- mechanical (ability to build, assemble, or construct)
- cultural/spiritual (knowledge and practices)

2. Make a list of the individuals who are already part of your life, and think about whether any these people could support you in additional ways—and how you can express your gratitude for what they've done for you already:
   - Who do you turn to when you need emotional support?
   - Do you have a person in your life that you talk to about values that ground you?
   - Who in your network of relationships shares an important identity with you?

3. Look through your social network connections to find one or more individuals who attend your college (or who know someone who does). Consider sending a private message to ask someone in your network a question or to see if they would be open to meeting with you to talk about your shared interests.

▾▾▼▾▾

PART II

You Never Know Who Will Change You (or How)

CHAPTER 4

Connecting with Peers

Find Your People

OF ALL THE RELATIONSHIPS you build in college, the ones you develop with your peers—with other students—are likely to be the most significant. We are not just saying that; researchers who study higher education have found that peer relationships matter a great deal.[1] The students we interviewed said the same thing. Anthony Mota, a LaGuardia Community College student and trained peer mentor, told us that college can feel like a place where you are being evaluated and graded all the time, but connecting with peers can give a person the chance "just to be themselves in a non-judgmental space. That can be really hard to find in college. It's important to just listen to their story because everybody's story here is different."

One of the benefits of college is that you are surrounded by students with diverse talents, interests, and identities. They are with you in class, whether you are meeting in person or virtually. Peers are learning assistants, tutors, leaders of student organizations and clubs, and perhaps even hanging out in the same places on social media or on campus that you do. These people could become your mentors and part of your professional network, or they may turn into lifelong friends who will invite you to their weddings. The students you connect with will be a defining feature of your college experience.

The peers you meet in your first year of college might be particularly important to you. A 2018 national poll that surveyed more than four thousand people who have earned associate's or bachelor's degrees found that almost 80 percent began their most significant college peer relationship during their first year, and most of these connections began in the classroom.[2] Who you talk to in class, who you study with, and who you interact with in online academic spaces will influence who you get to know. If you have already finished your first year and you have not yet found your people, the important thing is not to give up. Keep looking, especially in new or different spaces. Remember that each new class and experience is an opportunity to meet and interact with peers who might very well change your life for the better.

Peers will help you, support you, and challenge you in a variety of ways. Peer relationships in college tend to offer a mixture of supports: *well-being and emotional support* (including having fun!), *academic support* (learning), and *instrumental support* (practical, day-to-day living). Often students have different peers who fulfill each of these distinct roles—you might go out with one set of friends and study with another group. However, Dartmouth College professor of sociology Janice McCabe has shown that students who build the strongest peer relationships weave these three kinds of support together. In other words, in the strongest peer networks, students have relationships that offer them emotional, academic, *and* practical support.[3] Perhaps one of your

▼▼ ▼ ▼▼▼▼▼▼▼▼▼▼▼▼

"Lots of students go to class or an event, and then they leave or log out as soon as it ends. For me, just staying after a little bit to chat with other people really helped me find people who I have something in common with."

—Chloe Inskeep, University of Iowa

▲▲▲▲▲▲▲▲▲▲▲▲ ▲ ▲▲

goals can be to build this kind of powerful, long-lasting friendship with at least a few peers in college.

In this chapter, we explore those three categories of support your peers can provide. Additionally, we consider the impact negative peer relationships can have and show you examples of how students navigated these experiences.

Well-Being and Emotional Support

College is filled with moments of happiness, excitement, and joy. You also may experience times of stress, frustration, and anger. Being able to manage your mental and emotional well-being when things get tough will be important to your academic and personal success. You do not have to work through these feelings and experiences alone. During times of stress, your peers can be there to uplift and support you—and during joyful times, they can be there to celebrate with you and keep you grounded.

When Amber Musette Drew enrolled at Oakton Community College, she was determined to go "above and beyond" to open opportunities for herself and for her son. As a single mom, she had to juggle a lot of different priorities: childcare, a job, her classes, and leadership positions in student groups, including the Black Student Union. Her hard work paid off, and she made "a lot of great connections at Oakton." When she earned her degree and transferred to Northeastern Illinois University, however, she struggled with the transition from a community college where "professors, staff, and administrators were so loving, caring, and supportive" to a large and unfamiliar university where she had to start over and "felt super alone." Amber stayed connected with Oakton friends on Facebook and Instagram, but on her new campus she "did not really know what to do or where to fit in." Once again, Amber immersed herself in student organizations, and that helped her connect with people who would support her emotionally. At Northeastern Illinois, two peers in particular became "extremely meaningful and important" to her—Karen and Marchon:

> We talked all the time. They really helped me. I felt like I could be myself with both of them. For example, Karen knows all about my depression struggles and what it was like for me raising a kid. I have a sister who is disabled, and she does as well, so we connected through that. Being the sister of a sibling with a disability and having it on your shoulders growing up, caring for them, while also going to school and trying to find your own identity can be a lot. So Karen is my very best friend, and Marchon my supporter in everything I do. He is my biggest cheerleader. He's always on my Instagram, just like rooting me on.

▽▽▼▼▽▽▽▽▽▽▽▽▽▽▽

"When I think of peer advising, I think about my first peer advisor, Karla, and how she changed my life. She gave me the resources I needed to be part of the community and to be part of college. She assisted me with being part of the clubs that I wanted to be in and to be part of the Peer Advisor Academy as well, and motivated me in ways that no one else did. The first time we met, she was welcoming. She was warm. I guess she saw a little bit of herself in me, and me in her."

—Jessica Taurasi, LaGuardia Community College

▲▲▲▲▲▲▲▲▲▲▲▲▲▲ ▲ ▲▲

Throughout Amber's time at Northeastern Illinois, Karen and Marchon provided the well-being and emotional support she needed. They kept her "grounded" and allowed her the space to "be myself." She no longer felt like she "had to be superwoman all the time." She could simply be who she was and not feel like she "had to hide anything or had to be super strong all the time." After earning her degree from Northeastern Illinois, Amber moved to Nashville to go to graduate school at Vanderbilt University; she remained so close to Karen and Marchon (mostly through social media) that they both traveled to Nashville to be in her wedding.

Academic Support

Learning often occurs in relationship with others. Peers are essential partners in learning—in study groups, during class activities, working on problem sets, giving feedback on draft papers, and just talking through ideas. Often peers also have formal roles as learning assistants or tutors to help you learn and feel confident about complex course material.

When Nellie Bourne started a certified nursing assistant program at Lake Washington Institute of Technology, near Seattle, she was older than many of her classmates. Nellie sometimes felt she was surrounded by people who reminded her a lot of her 17-year-old self. She described some of these students as "not wanting to be there" and muttering under their breath ("This sucks.") when asked to talk in class. One day Nellie paired up with a peer who had a "horrible attitude. He didn't seem to know why he was there, and his grades were suffering." The student reminded her of her younger brother, so she decided to take him under her wing and help him academically. She talked to him before class, encouraged him to speak up in discussions, and invited him to study together before the next exam. Thanks to Nellie's support—and his own hard work—he went from failing almost all of his classes to

☑ **FACT:** **Giving gives back.** Scholars call what Nellie experienced "giver's gain" because college students who provide written feedback and other forms of academic support to their peers frequently end up seeing significant benefits to their own learning from the process.* What opportunities can you identify to offer support and feedback to your peers?

* Melissa Meeks, "Giver's Gain in Peer Learning," *Eli Review Blog*, March 28, 2017, https://elireview.com/2017/03/28/givers-gain/.

earning good grades that semester. Nellie was surprised to find that "encouraging and working with him actually improved my grades too," and she ended up with a 4.0 GPA that quarter.

When they both graduated from Lake Washington Institute of Technology, the two shared tears of joy because they were "super excited" for one another. Nellie's friend went on to earn a nursing degree at a four-year institution, and five years later they continue to be "best friends to this day." He still occasionally reminds Nellie that "I wouldn't be here if it wasn't for you."

Classrooms are not the only place students can academically support one another. In fact, learning from peers can take place just about anywhere online or on campus. At Hope College in Michigan, first-year students have the opportunity to participate in Day1 Research, a yearlong undergraduate research program that engages students in efforts to understand and improve the water quality in the Lake Michigan ecosystem. Throughout the year, Day1 students sometimes take the same classes and collaborate in teams to work outside of class on research projects. Many students in Day1 live in the same residence building: Lichty Hall (in chapter 7, you will read about how Lichty Hall combines several features of "relationship accelerator" experiences).

This residential learning community with peers is the "heart and soul" of Day1. Abby Pearch, a first-year student, described it as a "little family.... You see them every day, you can't avoid them, and you get to know everyone." Lichty Hall is a place where students' academic and social lives are woven together in ways that provide academic (and also emotional and practical) support. Abby told us, "In Lichty, you would walk downstairs, and everyone was doing homework. A lot of times people were working on the same thing, and if you had a question, you could find someone who could help you answer it. I was always there, surrounded by other students who were working on science too."

Because of the supportive academic community, Abby would usually do her homework in Lichty. Although college was academically challenging at times, Abby's peers helped her along the way—they even bonded over a particularly difficult chemistry class. After her first year in Day1, Abby realized research was not her calling, but the next year she lived with a couple of her friends from Lichty.

The Nepantla Program at Nevada State College is another powerful type of academic community designed to support the college journeys of bright, ambitious first-generation college students, many of whom have mastered English as a second language and hope one day to be United States citizens. Nepantla offers an opportunity to begin taking college courses before first-year fall enrollment (at some schools this is called a summer bridge program); intensive mentoring by professional staff, faculty, and peers; and most important, a deep sense of belonging and connection. Maria Balleza Franco, a double major in environmental and resource science and business administration with a minor in pre-law, participated in Nepantla as a student and later held leadership positions in the program as a peer mentor, intern, and course assistant. She reflects on what those connections meant to her as a first-year student:

I met my most important peers and friends through Nepantla and the space that we share—a place to come to and have lunch together. I think the main thing I learned from my peers initially was accountability—especially in the first year of college. When I didn't want to go to class or was dreading a class, my peers showed me that the main thing for success in college is just to show up for class—to be there and be engaged. And because those peers were in some of my classes, they were like, "Let's go. We have class!"

Practical (How-To) Support

The third kind of aid peers can provide is practical guidance about navigating college and living a busy life as a student. A peer may guide you through the course registration process, or talk you through how to find a job on campus, or even offer life-changing advice.

Brandon Bond, a student leader at the University of Michigan, knows well the impact peer relationships can have on students' college journey. In his first year, Brandon was a part of three university mentoring programs. After that year, his involvement with the programs inspired him to serve as a peer mentor and give back to first-year students. As a peer mentor, he remembers one interaction in particular:

> She was a pre-med student, and of course she was worried about completing all of these required classes; however, she really wanted to study abroad and worried she would never be able to do that because of her pre-med requirements. So one day I sat down with her at one of our cafés and pulled out a study abroad program catalog so we could narrow down her top program options. After doing so, she was then worried about money, so we made the whole budget for everything, and I suggested some scholarships she should apply for through the university. She eventually had a plan to pay for everything, to study abroad, and to stay in pre-med.

Thanks to Brandon's help, this student was able to fully fund her semester abroad in Japan. The relationship Brandon and his peer developed eventually grew, and they became good friends. She then invited Brandon to see her be initiated into her sorority. Later in college, the relationship had an unexpected benefit for Brandon. The two of them were in a class together, and Brandon was struggling: "I wasn't really sure what was going on for a lot of the semester," but his mentee "knew everything, and it all just clicked for her." His mentee then became the person who helped him in class. Their relationship evolved from a practical conversation about study abroad into one where each of them supported the other. Brandon realized that he did not have to have all the answers, but together, they could learn from each other and grow in tandem.

Olegaria Gonzalez, also a peer educator and intern in the Nepantla Program at Nevada State College, explains the simple but powerful support peer mentors can provide to new students:

> I saw that as new incoming students, they were as lost as I was. They didn't want to talk to anyone. They didn't know how to reach out to professors. They didn't know how to speak for themselves. But because I was one or two years older than them, I could help them navigate. I helped them find classes, use the learning management system and the student portal, and discover resources available to them. I was there as a friend and a mentor, and they trusted me, even with aspects of their personal lives.

Peer educators of all types—from friends to learning assistants in the classroom or resident assistants in a dorm—may be some of the most important people to help you figure out the complexities of college.

When Peer Relationships Go Wrong

Sometimes peer relationships do not develop the way you expect. Contrasting views, values, and beliefs—or damaging behavior—can produce tension or end friendships. Often, with reflection and thoughtful action, you can manage these experiences yourself. However, sometimes you may need help dealing with a situation, so talking with a trusted friend or professional (your advisor, a professor, a counselor) can be useful.

Like many first-year students, Kayla Neal, from the University of Michigan–Flint, expected to meet their best friend in college. Soon after moving to campus, feeling anxious about who that person could be, Kayla became inseparable from Lauren, a student who lived in the same residence hall. At first, the relationship flourished—the two ate, studied, and had fun together. When Kayla needed to go grocery shopping, they knew Lauren would give them a ride.

When discussing politics, however, Kayla began to notice fundamental differences in their views about the world. Kayla's identities and political views prompted them to ask questions that challenged Lauren's opinions. Sometimes these conversations heated up. One time, Kayla asked, "How are you going to have these beliefs that explicitly go against who I am as a person?" Kayla eventually told Lauren, "You are actively supporting someone and a cause that contradicts my entire existence." Kayla decided they had to break off the friendship, which was intensely painful. Kayla had invested so much time in the relationship and truly thought they had found a best friend. Since Kayla and Lauren shared the same friends, things remained awkward for a while, but eventually Kayla established a new friend group that was consistent with their identities and values.

Experiences like Kayla's are common in college. You are bound to meet and interact with peers from many different backgrounds who have a wide variety of perspectives and opinions. That diversity can be an important, exciting opportunity for growth and change. It can also lead to conflict. Separating from peers is sometimes necessary for your own emotional and academic well-being, and that is completely okay.

On the other hand, there is power in leaning into thoughts and ideas that challenge us. As a matter of fact, diverse perspectives and life experiences can allow us the opportunity to grow and further our relationships. For Moon Medina, a student majoring in international relations at Florida International University (FIU), conflict actually strengthened their relationship with a peer. Raised in a conservative town, Moon believed their upbringing had "stifled my growth as a human being." Only after arriving at FIU in Miami did Moon feel like they could be "my own person."

In one class, Moon connected with a peer who soon became one of their greatest friends. This friend was so caring that Moon could "go to this man for anything, he was the absolute best." As the friendship developed, Moon noticed that this friend would occasionally use anti-LGBTQ language. Assuming good intent, Moon wondered if their friend's comments were "something he believed or it was something they had been taught" and found the courage to talk to him about how his words were hurtful to Moon and others. That was a painful discussion, but he told Moon he would try to "broaden his perspective." Years later, they remain good friends, although they don't always agree politically.

Most peer interactions will not be as difficult as Kayla or Moon's or as rewarding as Brandon or Nellie's. Still, peer relationships will be the bedrock of your time in college. Build a strong foundation for yourself by reaching out to peers—even when that feels hard to do. Peers can offer you emotional, academic, and practical support, and you can do the same for them. As the stories in this chapter show, peer relationships sometimes can blossom from classroom chats into lifelong friendships. What can you do to start building connections with your peers?

Ask Yourself . . .

1. Name a peer you admire. What are the qualities of this person that you respect?

2. Do you have a friendship that supports you in a number of overlapping ways (academically, emotionally, practically)? How could you support your friends in overlapping ways?

3. What are three simple ways you can give greater attention to peer relationships? (Examples: put down your phone, use social media more strategically, invite a classmate for coffee after class.)

4. How could you extend relationships with peers in the classroom outside of class? (Examples: form study groups, set up a class group text.)

5. Have you ever had to reassess or cut off a friendship because it was not healthy? What did you learn about yourself from that experience?

6. How do you use social media to enhance meaningful peer relationships? In what ways might your social media use be more healthy?

7. Are your relationships with peers from high school—or other aspects of your life outside of college—nourishing or limiting?

Try This!

1. If you are doing most of your studying alone, try the benefits of a study group, where peers review material and teach each other. These scheduled meetings also help ensure you are devoting your time to academics.

2. Do you have a peer who supports you in more than one dimension of your life (well-being and emotional support, academic support, practical support)? Express gratitude to that person for being such an important friend.

3. Find a student who seems lonely or who appears to be ignored, and introduce yourself.

CHAPTER 5

Connecting with Professors
In and Out of Class

WHEN SAM OWUSU left home in Chicago to attend Davidson College, he wondered what life would be like as a Black man living on a predominately white campus in a suburb of Charlotte, North Carolina. His first few days went great as he got to know his peers and settled into his dorm. And when classes began, he jumped right in: "During my very first class, I was excited and nervous. I wanted to major in political science, and my professor was one of the big names in that department."

Looking back a few years later, shortly after graduating from Davidson, Sam still remembers how he felt as a new college student: "Yeah, it is intimidating. It's not an easy process of building relationships with people you consider to be some of the brightest people that you've ever met. You just have this feeling that you always have to be right about everything and this sense that you're an imposter. 'If I'm not right then I shouldn't be saying anything.'"

But then one day, when Sam struggled with a class project, the same "big name" professor emailed to ask, "Hey what's going on?" And she specifically asked "Are *you* okay?" first. "The project can come second, but are you okay?" Experiences like this one taught him that professors could care for him as a person, not just as a student. They have feelings just like you. They can have good days and not so good days, and some of them can tell when there is something wrong. Until you've interacted with them enough to know if they are not kind or not caring, assume they want you to succeed.

It is common for undergraduates to feel intimidated by professors, and that feeling tends to be particularly strong for students who have doubts about whether they belong in college. You might be wondering about this yourself. Despite these understandable apprehensions, the classroom—whether in person or online—is *the* place where most of your learning will happen in college. The interactions you have with your professors, and the relationships you build with them, can and will be transformational for you. Decades of research show that the quality of student-faculty relationships is one of the most important factors

"In high school, they made college seem to be the worst place to be, but it has been literally quite the opposite. I was so afraid to go to college, but clearly each university is different, and professors are different. But for the most part they want to help you learn. It's so refreshing knowing that it's different."

—Kayla Neal, University of Michigan–Flint

FACT: **Helping professors get to know you pays off.** Students who believe their professor knows their name and cares about their success are more likely to ask for help and to work hard to succeed.* Introduce yourself to your professor so they can learn your name, and don't be surprised if you need to remind them of your name later—many professors teach a *lot* of students.

* Katelyn M. Cooper et al., "What's in a Name? The Importance of Students Perceiving That an Instructor Knows Their Names in a High-Enrollment Biology Classroom," *CBE—Life Sciences Education* 16, no. 1 (March 1, 2017): ar8, https://doi.org/10.1187/cbe.16-08-0265.

in a whole range of positive experiences in and outcomes from college for all students, and especially for first-generation undergraduates and students of color.[1]

If you're just starting college and think it's too soon to start connecting with your professors, keep in mind that 60 percent of graduates in a national poll reported meeting their most influential college faculty or staff member during their first year.[2] Students usually meet these professors in their courses, meaning that the classroom experience, and particularly the first-year classroom experience, is pivotal.

None of these research findings make interacting with faculty easy, but they do suggest it will be important for you to devote time and effort to cultivating relationships with your professors. This chapter will help. We'll share stories of students connecting with faculty in ways that help them learn and be successful in college and that have long-term implications for their work and lives after graduation. You'll read about both in- and out-of-class connections between students and professors, including specific opportunities, like office hours, that can deepen your faculty relationships. The chapter concludes with some stories of negative student-faculty interactions and some advice about handling these.

Students (Yes, You) Are a Priority

At the beginning of this chapter, Sam already described one reason it can be hard to connect to professors: the perception that they might be "some of the brightest people that you've ever met." Other students were worried about interrupting faculty work. Growing up in Miami, Paula Lisazo knew she wanted to be a doctor, so she was a serious student—and she always did well in school. However, her science courses at Florida International University could be "intimidating." Paula says she had to get out of her comfort zone and get over the idea she would be bothering her professors by reaching out to them: "I don't like thinking I'm pestering teachers."

It's true that your professors have many responsibilities. These often include teaching, conducting research, providing leadership to their department and school, mentoring students, and much more. Some of them may teach full time at just one institution, while others may teach part time at multiple colleges. Some classes have graduate students who are instructors or teaching assistants, while others may be led by a professor with undergraduate students serving as learning assistants. Regardless of who is teaching the class or what other responsibilities they may have, that person is responsible for teaching your class, and as a student, you are one of their priorities. Paula says that over time she realized not only that she was *not* pestering her professors but that they appreciated it when she stayed in touch with them.

Connecting in the Classroom

Paula told us about another professor, one she liked so much she took three of his classes. But he did something during class that scared her at first: calling on a student by name to answer a question in front of everyone in a large lecture hall. After talking with him, she saw that he wanted to get to know his students, even in big classes: "If you went to his office hours, he'd answer your questions and learn your name. And he was so interested in your life— he always asked what other classes I was taking and what I hoped to do with my degree." If she saw him in the hallway before or after class, he'd greet her by name.

Slowly she came to realize that what at first made her nervous— his habit of asking specific students a question in class—was his way of checking in to see if everyone was understanding the material. When he'd ask in class, "'Hey Paula, what do you think of this?' I sometimes would say, 'I don't know,'" and he would then slow down. "If you didn't understand something, you always felt like you could tell him, and he'd help you learn."

Those kinds of connections might not surprise you for a student who took three in-person classes with the same professor, but what about online classes? When Nellie Bourne at San Antonio College signed up for a fully online required writing class, she did not think she would interact much with her professor. Nellie struggled to balance school with her job and her home life (including her husband and two active dogs) during the pandemic, and she worried that having to write two papers a week for this class would feel like a chore. However, the professor gave her such helpful, prompt, and affirming feedback on her writing that she found herself working extra hard: "On some papers, she would have this little paragraph in the comments saying, 'You did this super well in your paper,' and that little bit of encouragement, even though you're not face-to-face with this teacher at all, made a world of difference to me." Nellie appreciated her professor's feedback so much that she took a second course with her, even though she wasn't required to do so. Although they have *never* met in person or spoken to each other, Nellie insists this professor "has made a huge, a positive difference" for her—which, she notes, "is kind of hard to do when you're not actually interacting with students in a classroom or on Zoom."

Other students connected with professors who share aspects of their identities or passions. Lance Lindsay developed his strongest faculty relationship with Professor Valerie Johnson, the chair of the political science department at DePaul University, who knew Lance intended to go to graduate school: "She sometimes took a hard stance toward me. She would ask, 'Do you know the

Small Steps to Connect with Your Professor

Here are some basic strategies to begin building a relationship with any professor:

1 Read the syllabus, which explains course content and procedures like homework and grading. If you still have questions about the course after you've read the syllabus, ask the professor. Start your email or comment to them with something like "Would you please help me understand this part of the syllabus?" or "I have a question that I didn't see answered in the syllabus."

2 Be ready to participate and be engaged in every class. Do the reading and the homework. Ask a question or join in classroom discussion, and use technology (your phone, a laptop) only for educational activities in class—and as described in the syllabus. And come to class! If you absolutely must arrive late or be absent, email your professor letting them know and asking what you need to do to make up any work that you miss.

3 Communicate with your professor if you are having difficulty with (or are excited about) the course material or if you will be late with an assignment. Sometimes professors are willing to provide a deadline extension if you communicate with them in advance. Do not "ghost" your professor, leaving them wondering why you have missed class or not submitted assignments. Let them know what is happening with you, and oftentimes you will find that moment can become an important point of connection for the two of you.

percentage of people of color in higher education? Your work needs to be tight.'" Similarly, Jennyflore Andre felt drawn to Professor Sat Gavassa, a biological sciences professor at Florida International University, because "I saw similar traits in the two of us. She has a little shyness about her, and she works hard to do everything perfectly."

Connections That Challenge and Support

Part of why effective professors contribute so much to students' college experiences is that they both challenge *and* support them. This echoes the research about what the best college teachers do.[3] In our interviews, we heard this over and over from students who described their favorite professors as the ones who knew them well enough to push them academically and to encourage and believe in them personally. Sophie Danish, a history major at Davidson College, said of her favorite professor: "By challenging me, not just handing over a grade, she was demonstrating that she really wanted to help me improve. And I decided that I really wanted to impress her with my work." Tajhae Barr, a recent graduate of the University of Michigan–Flint and a published author, teared up as she recalled her first-semester writing professor, who had high standards for her students. "At first I thought she was indifferent toward freshmen," but over the semester Tajhae realized her professor was doing her best to prepare first-generation students like her to be successful in their classes: "She wanted us to understand what was going to be required of us throughout our academic and professional careers, and she wanted us to know she believed we were capable of developing our learning and writing skills to distinguish ourselves."

Sometimes Professors Help You See Yourself

Peta-Gaye Dixon, a former student success mentor at LaGuardia Community College, recalls how two conversations led to her decision to pursue a career as a teacher. She entered LaGuardia intending to study business so she could support her mother back home in Jamaica; she never imagined herself in education because she had struggled with ADHD (attention deficit hyperactivity disorder) throughout her years of schooling:

> Professor Silverman, my psychology professor, told me: "Peta, your papers are terrific. Why don't you go into education?" I'm like, "Me, teaching children? I can't teach anybody. I barely made it through school. I can't do that." Professor Silverman replied, "Think about it." The next day I got a copy of an email from her to a professor in the education department. It said, "I might have found you an excellent teacher candidate." I decided to follow Professor Silverman's advice, so I went to see Professor Cornelia in education, who told me she also had ADHD. She sat me down in her office and showed me all her credentials on her wall, and she said, "I am you. And look where I am. You are going to be a great educator because you know what these kids are going through." And then she asked me to sit down in her chair behind her desk, and she said, "You're in the professor's chair. That's your master's on the wall. That's your PhD. How are you going to tell me you can't do it? You're going to be a great teacher."

Not only did these two conversations with Professors Silverman and Cornelia change Peta's life, but they will also ripple through classrooms for years to come as she teaches and mentors her own students.

Karey Frink of Hope College was struggling so much in her chemistry course that she was thinking of dropping the class. Her professor, Dr. Peaslee, found out about this and asked her to talk. Karey says, "I was shaking in my boots. I have to confront my super smart professor and tell him that I'm failing chemistry." But when they met, he spoke about her strengths and said, "Karey, I see you having skills that others in the class don't have, like communication skills, understanding the basics of how science works and being able to communicate it in layman's terms." Karey became a communications major, inspired by what Professor Peaslee identified in her.

Office Hours Are *Student* Hours

You have many chances to interact informally with faculty, both during class and by "just staying after class to chat sometimes," to borrow a strategy from Chloe Inskeep, a student at the University of Iowa. Perhaps the easiest opportunity to connect with faculty outside of class is during office hours—sometimes called student hours or other names. During office hours, which tend to be listed on the course syllabus, faculty are available for drop-in conversations with students. You don't need an appointment or even a formal reason for stopping by a professor's office hours. Professors set aside this time specifically to meet with students. If you cannot make the times listed, email your professor to ask if there are other times they are available. In addition, teaching assistants (TAs, who are usually graduate students) often have office hours for students, which can be particularly helpful if you're in a class that has a lot of students.

Office Hours 101

You might never have heard of "office hours" before college. Here are four things you need to know:

1 **Office hours are *student* hours.** Bryan Dewsbury, a biology professor at Florida International University, found that some students thought the term "office hours" meant that was the time professors were in their offices getting their work done. He renamed them "student hours" to clear up their purpose. No matter what your professor calls them, office hours are for you.

2 **Office hours don't always take place in professors' offices.** Professor Dewsbury often holds "student hours" in a residence hall to make it easier for students to attend and so there will be more space for a crowd—because many students tend to stop by. Professors who teach online courses, and sometimes professors who teach on-campus courses, will have office hours virtually (for example, on Zoom) to make it convenient to connect.

3 **You don't have to go alone.** Professor Dewsbury encourages his students to attend office hours in groups. Students will respond to one another's questions and work together to solve problems. Even if your professor does not explicitly mention visiting office hours in pairs or groups, feel free to go together with another student from your class.

4 **Office hours are also a time to ask questions beyond the course material.** You might be interested in talking about choosing a major, pursuing undergraduate research, or other bigger questions, from internship or community service possibilities to career or life advice.

The key is to actually go to office hours (online or in person), and ideally to go early in the semester. Research suggests that new students who go to office hours during the first three weeks of the semester are more likely than their peers to be successful academically.[4]

Despite the benefits, for many students fear can make office hours seem daunting. Abraham Segundo, who returned to college for a second time after initially withdrawing, described his own experience this way:

> At first, I was scared of teachers because I was worried about what they would think if I asked them questions or showed them that I didn't understand something. But in reality, they're here to help. I didn't see that when I was younger. Now I know that teachers will spend time with you to help you learn; you just have to ask. Now that I'm back in school, every chance I get, I ask a question in class or I'll go to office hours.

Like Abraham, Paula Lisazo was apprehensive about going to see a professor, but one of her first-year professors encouraged all his students to visit office hours, so she did: "He was friendly, and he asked me how the semester was going overall. We didn't only talk about the class because he wanted to know a bit about me as a person." For Paula, that interaction convinced her that she could—and should—go to office hours with other faculty, "so it was a good start for me developing relationships with professors even though I'm at a huge school taking mostly big classes."

▼▼▼▼▼▼▼▼▼▼▼▼▼▼▼▼▼

"Professors love to answer questions. That's their job."

—Amena Shukairy, University of Michigan–Flint

▲▲▲▲▲▲▲▲▲▲▲▲▲▲▲▲▲

You do not have to be a student in a professor's course to visit their office hours. Sam Owusu spent his first year "talking to almost every professor in the political science department" to figure out who he wanted to be his advisor.

Also keep in mind that you don't have to stay for an hour or even a half hour to benefit from office hours. Even a brief visit can help. At Oakton Community College, faculty who participate in the Persistence Project meet one on one with each student for a ten-minute conversation during the first three weeks of the semester. Oakton students, particularly those who are new to higher education, report being "intimidated" and "kind of scared" by the requirement to meet individually with faculty. However, Allison Wallin, who is studying environmental science, explained that "having to have that meeting creates a relationship that you can build on later in the semester if you ever need to talk to them about a problem. And it makes it easier to speak up in class." Gina Roxas, a student planning to transfer to earn her bachelor's degree in biology, describes one such meeting with a professor as "very key to my education here because she not only showed that she cared about her students but also was well versed in the resources available to support students, which helped me connect with the honors program and a science mentor and also scholarship opportunities."

FACT: **You need your professors to remember you.** Students routinely ask faculty to serve as a reference for a job or to write a letter of recommendation for a scholarship or application. Be sure you have gotten to know the faculty you might ask for a reference or recommendation so that they can be knowledgeable advocates for you.

The connections you establish in office hours often won't last beyond the semester, but sometimes you will have begun to build the kind of relationship that can blossom into advising and mentoring. Students like Paula who hope to attend graduate or professional school, for example, will need letters of recommendation, and the best letters are written by faculty who know you.

Other students discover their academic passions in office hours. Wren Renquist entered the University of Iowa intending to go to medical school, but a required botany unit in an introductory biology course sparked her curiosity: "I loved that botany section so much, I continuously went to her office hours. At the end of the semester, I knew her and her research well enough that I asked if I could join her lab—and she knew me well enough to say yes!"

Relationship Challenges with Professors

Student-faculty relationships are powerful, even transformative. They also can go wrong. You should not tolerate sexual harassment, racial abuse, or other forms of discrimination in education. It is unacceptable, illegal, and immoral. If something like this happens to you, immediately contact an official at your college; if you don't know who to speak to, start with the provost's or dean's office. These administrators have broad responsibility for students and education—they will know how to support and assist you.

It's more likely that you'll come across faculty who are not (or *appear* not to be) responsive to their students or not connecting meaningfully with them. In our interviews with undergraduates across the country, we heard many inspiring stories of amazing teaching, but we also heard about a professor who promised to make sure many students didn't pass their class and a first-year writing professor who collected their students' first assignments and then—without even reading them—walked to the front of the room and threw those papers in the trash, saying, "I know you guys can do better than this."

What should you do? Believe it or not, sometimes the best thing you can do in this situation is go to the professor's office hours, introduce yourself, and ask a few questions about the class. Once you begin to build a relationship with the professor, you'll be able to judge what your next step should be—perhaps the professor was trying (and failing) to make an important point about their class, or maybe they are not interested in the needs of students. If you think they don't have your education at heart, then you might need to talk to your academic advisor or the department chair or academic dean to ask for advice about whether to switch to another section of the course.

Sometimes *students* make mistakes that can damage student-faculty relationships. Brandon Daye, a supply chain management and agribusiness management double major at North Carolina A&T, told us about a big mistake he made his first semester:

> I got so involved in football and campus life that I only went to my English class a couple of times throughout the semester. On the last day of the class, I showed up with all my work for the whole course. When everyone left, I went up to the professor and handed her my work. She looked at me and said, "No. I cannot accept this or allow you to pass. That's not fair to other students, and you won't learn from this experience." I was heartbroken. She told me, "Brandon, you fell down, but you can get back up. You need to decide what you want and then focus on that." That's why I ended my first semester with a 1.94 GPA. I was struggling. Now I can gladly say I have a 3.51 GPA, and I am interning at two

places. I learned so much from having to figure out what mattered to me.

As Brandon discovered, mistakes are almost always powerful teachers.

Katy, a strategic communications major at Elon University, also stumbled in her first year. During her second semester, she was disappointed and frustrated with the B she earned on an exam, so she changed one of her answers: "I abandoned logic and moral reasoning and approached my professor for two small percentage points. I walked into Professor Landesberg's office and lied to him, showing him his 'mistake' where he had marked my answer as wrong." What Katy did not know is that her professor kept copies of all student exams; he had proof that she had cheated. He quickly informed her that cheating meant she would earn an F in the course. Katy was devastated, but she decided to demonstrate to Professor Landesberg—and herself—that she could recover from this grave mistake. She attended every day of this class the rest of the semester, turning in all the assigned work and studying hard for the final exam. After the semester ended, she asked Professor Landesberg to be her academic advisor and he agreed. Katy says that one of the highlights of her college experience was his telling her "I'm proud of you" as she prepared for graduation three years later. Katy still needed to repeat her failed class, but she counts this experience among the most powerful learning experiences of her life—and she considers Professor Landesberg her most important mentor in college.

Not every student is lucky enough to encounter a professor like Katy's, but all students can interact with faculty who can be long-term mentors—or mentors-of-the-moment (see chapter 8). Many faculty are eager to build this kind of educational relationship with you. Open yourself up to this possibility by, like Sam

Owusu said at the beginning of this chapter, being willing to take the risk of asking or answering a question in class, chatting with a professor after class, going to office hours, or inquiring about the possibility of undergraduate research or other academic experiences outside of class. In Sam's words, "I think the first step that I made in building a relationship with professors was being okay with being wrong and admitting that I don't know the answer to everything. That meant I had to get used to being vulnerable in that moment" of asking a question, sending an email, or stopping by office hours. Small steps like these can make all the difference in your education as you build relationships with your professors.

Of course, you are not likely to make a meaningful connection with every single faculty member who teaches you. Still, you might be surprised to find that a professor in a required course— or one who seems very different from you—is eager to support and challenge you. Nellie Bourne had that experience in her writing course. Sometimes our most significant relationships emerge unexpectedly. Be open to and on the lookout for ways to interact with your professors—which can be as simple as participating actively in class. If all you do is help your professor learn your name, you've established a foundation that you can build on when you have questions or need help in class. And you may begin a relationship that will inspire you to learn in ways you never thought possible.

 Ask Yourself . . .

1. If you need to contact a professor, how would you reach out? How would you write that email? Do you know how your professor prefers to be addressed? (When in doubt, use "Professor ____.")

2. Who are your favorite professors—or what are your favorite classes—this year? Would you consider talking to one (or more) of those professors before or after class about what interests and excites you about the course?

3. What are three to five questions you could ask your professor during office hours that are not directly course related? (For example: How did you decide to become a professor? What was the most important thing you did in college to be successful? Did you experience homesickness when you were in college?)

 ## Try This!

1. Find out when one of your professors has office hours by checking the course syllabus. Before you stop by or virtually attend their office hours, write down a couple of questions and bring them with you.

2. Introduce yourself to your professor during one of the first few days of class. You might tell them your name, where you are from, your major or class year (for example, first-year or sophomore), and one thing you are looking forward to in the course.

3. Practice writing an email. Below is one example of how you could write an email to a professor. Yours does not have to look like this, but emails generally follow this format: (1) "Hi Professor ____," or "Hi Dr. ____,"; (2) introduce yourself if the professor does not know you; (3) state your reason for reaching out; and (4) close with something like "Sincerely, [your name]."

Hi Professor Smith,

I hope you are doing well. My name is Oscar Miranda Tapia, and I am a first-year student in your Introduction to Psychology class that meets on Tuesdays and Thursdays at 9:30 a.m.

I am reaching out because I am having some trouble understanding the class material, and my job and class schedule do not allow me to attend your office hours. Are there other days and times you are available to talk through some of the questions I have?

Thank you for your time and consideration.

Sincerely,
Oscar Miranda Tapia

CHAPTER 6

Connecting
with Staff
Allies Everywhere

WHEN WE ASKED Ruth Moreno from San Antonio College about her most meaningful relationships in college, she told us about two of her advisors, Jim Lucchelli and Bertha Castellanos. Even though they both support hundreds of students through their positions, "when you're sitting in front of them, they make you feel like the world has stopped and they're only focused on you," Ruth told us. Other students shared stories of relationships with academic advisors, dining hall workers, student life professionals, athletics staff, and more. At many institutions, for every *one* professor there are *two* individuals who work in a non-teaching role—from librarians, technology experts, student life professionals, plumbers, and landscapers, to physical and mental health care professionals, tutors, and office assistants. It takes all of them to make a college run smoothly.

How can staff facilitate your success in college and even be some of your most important mentors? That is the focus of this chapter. We will profile a few key staff positions that are common at many colleges, and we hope you'll develop relationships with people in these and many other roles. When you look, you will find allies and mentors everywhere.

Advisors: Your College GPS

Ivette Perez is a student at City Tech, part of the City University of New York. The first time she met her academic advisor, David Latimer, Ivette told us that he welcomed her in a very warm way. "I really didn't expect it from an advisor or any staff member, because high school is kind of nonpersonal," she shared. "And the first thing he said was, 'How are you today?' And that meant a lot to me, because not many people take the time to find out how you are doing."

When we asked Sophie Danish, a history major at Davidson College, to think about meaningful college relationships, the first person who came to her mind was her advisor for her history major, a "brilliant" African history professor. Sophie appreciated her advisor's empathy and the chance to connect to an adult in a meaningful way: "I felt like she was a cool person to connect with, and since declaring my major and working with her, she's always helped me navigate lots of different things throughout college."

Sophie's use of the word "navigate" is an excellent way to think about what advisors do and can help you with. Virginia Union University professor of education Terrell Strayhorn uses the term "cultural navigators" to describe academic advisors. "Cultural" because colleges and universities have their own cultures (including their own language, values, norms, traditions, and rules), and "navigators" because advisors use their deep knowledge of college culture to help students make their way through education and life. Strayhorn compares advisors to tools like Google Maps or Waze:

Like a high-tech global positioning system or "GPS,"
cultural navigators do more than merely tell someone
where to go; they show them via demonstration, illustra-
tion, or simulation of possible paths. Cultural navigators
in higher education help guide students until they arrive
at their academic destination or at least until they are
comfortable steering while their cultural navigators act as
guides on the side and keep them on their path.[1]

Sometimes advisors work within specialized programs. At
Oakton Community College, we spoke to Amber Musette Drew,
who was part of a TRIO program, one of many initiatives supported by the U.S. federal government to help provide services for
students with financial and academic challenges that could get in
the way of their educational progress. In Amber's case, she says
TRIO advisor Joe Palencia changed her life. "He was my mentor
and one of the first people that I actually made connections with
in college," Amber recalls. "And he was really great with helping
me organize my time and connecting me to work-study opportunities. I had no idea about work-study, so he helped me get a job on
campus." He also connected her to an emerging leaders program,
which, in her words, "helps students get out of their shells and be
a little bit more confident and step into leadership roles."

Part of the reason academic advisors can make such a difference for you is that your relationship with them will often span
multiple semesters or years. They might partner with you to deter-
mine which classes to take and how to register, give you advice on
your major or career goals, help you work through challenges with
changing life circumstances, and prepare you for opportunities like
internships and study abroad. Over time, your advisor will get to
know you and come to understand your aspirations, strengths, and

fears—and you will become increasingly comfortable reaching out when you need help or advice.

Your Allies and Advocates: Student Support Staff

You will find many college offices to support student success. Sometimes the name of the program might not make it clear that it's a space for students like you, but you will find allies in the library, career center, residential life office, civic engagement and service-learning programs, counseling and health centers, campus recreation and outdoor programs, judicial affairs offices, departments for students with disabilities, and offices that support student identities, such as LGBTQ or multicultural student centers. Many colleges also have specialized programs for first-generation college students (like TRIO), tutoring and academic success coaching, and writing centers. No matter what these offices (or others) are called at your college, the important thing is that these places are focused on your success and are staffed by dedicated, professional experts who are anxious to engage with you.

The most effective of these programs provide a comprehensive web of support services to facilitate student success, oftentimes led by professional staff members who represent the "heart and soul" of the program because of their deep commitment to student success. In the Nepantla Program at Nevada State College introduced in chapter 4, program coordinator Johanna Araujo was pivotal to Maria Balleza Franco:

> She went way beyond her job description, I am sure. She would take the time to be genuine, and she was really interested in what we had to say. She would remember

things and ask, "How did that go?" She was also a first-generation college student, so she could see a lot of the struggles we had to go through that our parents did not understand. More than anything, it's a very hopeful experience when she tells you about her story, because you know you will be okay.

Nepantla's director Leilani Carreño told us that Maria's experience is no accident; the program is designed to combine high expectations for success, built-in mentoring by professionals and peers, and leadership development training:

We expect that once you are in this program to be part of the Nevada State community, and you will have mentorship through this program through the date of graduation. We make sure that students know that this is not just a summer bridge program but a four-year support program for them to grow and develop as students and student leaders on campus.

More Than a Boss

Working an on-campus job can help you connect more fully to your college—and campus employment has even been correlated with earning higher grades.[2] Several students, like Amber earlier in this chapter, told us that their on-campus job supervisors were an unexpected yet essential source of support. Even when your campus job is not connected to your career aspirations, your work supervisor and colleagues can help you develop important professional skills.[3]

University of Michigan–Flint senior and political science major Kayla Neal described their on-campus supervisor as one of their most meaningful college connections. Kayla has worked as a peer educator with Sarah Devit, the sexual as-sault advocate at the Center for Gender and Sexuality, for about a year and a half. "Honestly, she doesn't even act like my boss sometimes. She's just a really great person to be around, and she's really helped me throughout COVID, also with my job and stuff." She has consistently been someone Kayla knows they can lean on: "It's really comforting to know that she's there for me when I need her."

Aigné Taylor, who double majors in political science and sociology at North Carolina A&T State University, said she was not looking for a men-tor or job; she wanted to use her passion for civic and voter engage-ment and get more involved her sophomore year. But while attend-ing an off-campus conference, she bonded with Tiffany Seawright, the director of A&T's Office of Leadership and Civic Engagement, as they each sampled vegan snacks. Aigné eventually began work-ing for the center, and Seawright became her mentor, advisor, and "like a big sister; I call her auntie." Their relationship was strength-ened through their intense collaboration on developing programs for voter engagement: "The mentorship, the advice, the late-night talks, just me going into her office and being able to tell her how I'm feeling as a student and talk to her about so many different things that are affecting me as a young Black woman and also regarding A&T." All of this has shaped her both academically and personally. As Aigné puts it, "I wouldn't be the student leader or the young Black woman that I am without her mentorship and her guidance."

For Elon University third-year law student James Donnell, staff members offered critical support on his journey to become a

"People here see stuff in me that I don't see in myself. When I second-guess my ability to do something, my job supervisor, Ellen Quish, will say, 'Peta, what are you talking about? You're great at that,' or 'You should work on this.' When I'm struggling, I remember that Ellen told me I'm awesome. So I'm awesome."

—Peta-Gaye Dixon, LaGuardia Community College

lawyer. James was an Odyssey scholar at Elon, a program for high-achieving first-generation college students, and the program's director, Marcus Elliott, got to know him well over four years. Then, years later Elliott ended up being a character reference for James's application for admittance to the bar (a requirement to practice law). At Elon, James also held a job in the Phoenix Card services office, which issues Elon identification cards. James told us his supervisor, Janet Rauhe, had a big influence on him as an undergraduate. "She really took a liking to me and an interest in my success. Every time an attorney would come into the office, she would be intentional and introduce me to them." Your supervisor can provide far more than job assignments and a paycheck, as important as those are. Good supervisors will take an interest in your future

Don't hesitate to contact a counselor. At most colleges and universities, you'll find professional counselors—individuals who provide free and confidential one-on-one or group counseling and programming for students on topics such as loneliness, depression, anxiety, eating disorders, stress, alcohol or drug dependence, and wellness. If you think you're the only one feeling anxious or depressed, you most definitely are not: a 2021 national study found that almost half of the college students surveyed showed signs of depression and/or anxiety.*

Not only is the discussion with a counselor confidential (with only a few exceptions), but most colleges will require your permission to let anyone know you used a counseling service. A quick search on your college website will help you find out what's available, including group and online counseling. We encourage you to find and contact a counselor for general support or for help during a crisis, to learn coping skills, or to proactively work on your overall wellness.

*Nardy Baeza Bickel, "Anxiety, Depression Reached Record Levels among College Students Last Fall," University of Michigan News, February 25, 2021, https://news.umich.edu/anxiety -depression-reached-record-levels-among-college-students-last-fall/.

career, give you increasing responsibilities over time, coach you in professional skills that will help you be successful in the workplace, and be a source of continuing welcome and encouragement.

Lean on a College Leader

Your college also has leaders with the titles of dean, department chair, vice president, provost, director, and many more. We talked with a few students like Brian Chan who connected with a leader at their college. Brian is a recent graduate of DePaul University who works in management consulting. He began his college career at Oakton Community College and one year into his studies was elected to be a student trustee (boards of trustees at universities and colleges are made up of individuals who work with—and oversee—the president and who partner with top college leaders to approve policies and develop strategic plans, manage the budget, and often help with fundraising). Because of his position, Brian had the chance to meet Oakton president Joianne Smith as well as the many trustees who served on the board.

An only child who was raised by a single mother, Brian was devastated when his mom passed away while he was attending Oakton. Much to his surprise, at his mom's funeral "among the first people to show up were Trustee Martha Burns and President Smith." Brian told us that "one of the favorite things that my mom liked to eat was Italian beef." To honor Brian's mom, "Martha cooked Italian beef and served it to everyone after the funeral, and she stayed from beginning to

"My leadership is shaped by my own experience as a student coming from a low-income family with parents who were not college going. Relationships with my faculty and administrators as an undergraduate student shaped my thinking about my future and gave me the confidence to look beyond the limits I had set for myself and to go on and earn a PhD and to think about higher education as a career."

—Chancellor Harold Martin,
North Carolina A&T State University

end. That emotional support was really, really beneficial to me." Brian said that this experience at an extremely difficult moment in his life is a good example of how President Smith and Trustee Burns shaped his college experience: "For me, that was what the support from those two was like and helped me get through pretty much to graduation."

Leaders may have impressive titles, but they are people just like you, and chances are, they would love to get to know you. Most have committed their careers to education because they enjoy spending time with students and would be interested in hearing about your experiences. Sometimes these leaders might be able to introduce you to other professionals or connect you with experiences that will enrich your college journey, so do not hesitate to arrange a conversation. Always remember that the college exists *for you*, and you are a priority, not an imposition. You can reach out to campus leaders simply by introducing yourself at an event, approaching leaders on their walks on campus, or sending an email requesting an opportunity for a conversation.

Campus Heroes Everywhere

You will find talented and kind people on your campus who make your sandwich in the dining hall, clean the building where you study late at night, shovel the walks so you can get to class safely, and respond to a 911 call in an emergency. What you might not anticipate is that one of these individuals might become a mentor, confidant, or listening ear when you need it most. You should approach every staff member on your campus as someone who has the potential to teach you something important about life.

Timothy K. Eatman, dean of the Honors Living-Learning Community at Rutgers University–Newark and coauthor of the afterword to this book, has built an exceptional program that weaves staff-student interactions into everything from admissions interviews to day-to-day life on campus. He and his colleagues know how important it is for students to see familiar faces and to hear friendly words every day on campus. He also told us a story about an unexpected but powerful student-staff mentoring moment. Dean Eatman's daughter Jamila is a student at Spelman College in Atlanta. Once when she was having a particularly bad day, Jamila was sitting alone in the cafeteria: "One of the staff walked up to her and said, 'It's tough, baby, but you can do it.' And then she asked, 'Baby, are you a praying child?' When Jamila nodded, they sat down and prayed together in the cafeteria. That was so comforting to Jamila, and she never would have thought to ask someone on the staff for something like that." You might have responded differently in Jamila's situation, but the offer from the cafeteria staff demonstrated a sincere interest in this student's well-being.

Ayanna McConnell, who helps lead the alumni office at the University of Michigan, illustrates another way unanticipated student-staff interactions can be transformative. McConnell met a first-generation Michigan undergraduate who aspired to be a dentist and used her professional network to support this student: "My program has a board member and Michigan alum who is a dentist. I told him a bit about this student, and then I made sure she came to a networking event, where I introduced the two of them. They have been in contact ever since, and he has been integral in her career path."

At your college, many people are eager to help you learn, grow, and connect academically, professionally, and personally. Staff in all sorts of roles will be there for you on bad days—and good ones. You do not have to wait for them to come to you. Seek out connections with the staff you encounter. You will find allies and champions who will help you succeed.

Ask Yourself . . .

1. Who have been your most important allies, mentors, and advisors in college so far? Has one been a staff member? What sorts of things do you talk about? What are the most important things you have learned from them?

2. Do you have a job on or off campus? What are you learning from your supervisor? Have you discussed how your supervisor discovered their career?

3. What one simple step could you take to get to know a staff member (and potential mentor) better?

Try This!

1. Walk into your college library and ask a librarian about the resources and services available through the library. (While you're there, hang around. It's a great place to study and meet people.) Many college librarians teach, and most of them partner with professors to find ways to deepen your learning and teach important skills like information literacy. If you're a fully online student or not yet ready to talk in person, try chatting with a librarian virtually, whether through a chat function on the library website or by sending a quick email to a librarian.

2. Check out student support services on your campus website (such as career services, academic advising, counseling

services, and financial aid), and make an in-person or online visit to at least one to explore a question or interest.

3. Schedule some time to talk with your academic advisor so you can get to know each other before planning your next semester's schedule of classes. It's helpful for your advisor to know about your interests and goals.

PART III

▼▼▼▼▼

You Can Do It

CHAPTER 7

Relationship Accelerators

IN THE LAST THREE CHAPTERS you've read about why and how interactions with peers, professors, and college staff can contribute to your learning and well-being in college. The final three chapters of the book invite you to think about *what you can do* to make your education relationship rich. Remember, your college has many people and programs to support you in that work; you're not on your own. And again, it's the quality, not the quantity, of the relationships you develop in college that not only can help you succeed but can have long-term benefits for you, contributing to your career success and your civic engagement after you graduate—and even making it more likely you'll thrive personally throughout your life.[1]

This chapter shows how certain experiences called high-impact practices (or HIPs) can be particularly significant, even transformational, for students in college. These include internships, study abroad, undergraduate research, first-year seminars, and learning communities. We call these experiences "relationship accelerators" because that's what they do: they supercharge the educational interactions you have with peers, professors, staff, and community members. You should be alert to opportunities to engage in these experiences because they could be some of the most engaging and meaningful things you do in college.

Research demonstrates the many benefits of these practices for students, including greater engagement, deeper learning, and increased likelihood of graduating. These experiences are relationship accelerators in part because they immerse students in circumstances that offer both challenge *and* support. Sometimes these are classroom-based experiences, such as a first-year seminar or a senior capstone course. Other times, they take place off campus at internship sites (in business and government settings, for example) or through civic engagement experiences with community partners (such as weekly tutoring of children in reading at a local school). Importantly, many HIPs require students to apply their academic knowledge to real-world settings.[2] Research demonstrates that HIPs are meaningful for all students, and they tend to be particularly significant for first-generation undergraduates and students of color.[3]

How Can You Find Relationship Accelerators?

Many colleges have programs designed to help students find and engage with these high-impact practices.[4] Table 7.1 lists a few of the most common ones, including an explanation of how each can be a relationship accelerator for you. That list is *not* complete. You will encounter other relationship accelerators in college. Peer leadership roles, such as being a resident assistant in a residence hall or a peer tutor in a course or serving

"Everyone's experience is different, but for me, getting involved with student government was the number-one thing because joining something automatically gave me a way to meet people that I have something in common with."

—Amena Shukairy, University of Michigan–Flint

TABLE 7.1 High-Impact Practices and How They Accelerate Relationships

HIGH-IMPACT PRACTICE	HOW THIS HIP ACTS AS A RELATIONSHIP ACCELERATOR
First-year seminars	Interact intensely with faculty and new students in a small class.
Study abroad / study away	Meet and study with peers and others from a different culture.
Capstone projects and experiences	Connect what you have learned in college to produce something significant, guided by faculty and often collaborating with peers.
Internships	Connect with supervisors and coworkers in a professional setting.
Writing-intensive classes	Write for a real audience, and give peers feedback on their writing.
Undergraduate research	Pursue an intensive research or creative project while being mentored by a faculty expert.
Service and community-based learning	Partner with people to apply and develop your academic knowledge and skills to challenges that matter to the community.
Learning communities	Collaborate with other students, including peer leaders, to explore shared academic interests. These can be classroom or residentially based.

in student government, often have these characteristics. Participating in athletics, whether at the intercollegiate, club, or intramural level, puts you into intense relationships with peers and coaches who are working toward a shared goal. Throughout this book you've read about other examples, including campus employment and student clubs. You also can turn almost any in-depth college experience into a relationship accelerator if you intentionally seek to build connections with the people alongside you.

You *Can* Pursue Relationship Accelerators

For many students, the idea of pursuing an internship, studying for a semester in another city or country, asking a faculty member to be your research mentor, or becoming a leader of a student organization seems daunting. If you are working long hours outside of school, or are studying fully online, or are a parent, or are the first in your family to go to college, these experiences may seem unattainable. However, relationship accelerators are in your reach if you do two things:

1. **Develop a relational mindset.** Many colleges are embedding high-impact practices directly in the curriculum, so you likely will experience relationship accelerators in some of the courses you take, such as a required first-year seminar, a capstone experience, or a writing-intensive course in your major. Sometimes, though, students don't fully embrace these potentially powerful opportunities. Group work can be difficult to manage on a busy schedule, but if you approach the assignment and your peers with a relational mindset, you'll be more likely to learn some of the interpersonal skills that will serve you well even after you graduate (like collaboratively working toward deadlines and giving constructive feedback to peers), as well as earn a better grade.

2. **Plan ahead.** Studying abroad, completing an internship, or conducting undergraduate research usually requires substantial preparation. To make these opportunities possible, plan early, seek expert guidance, and apply for funding to support the extra costs that some of these experiences may entail. This will require action on your part, but we believe

that if you can take the first concrete step toward your goal—sending an email, setting up a meeting, attending an information session—you will be surprised by how many people will want to help you realize your dreams.

Remember, quality is more important than quantity. Participating in just one or two high-quality HIPs can have a huge impact on your college experience.

Classroom-Based Relationship Accelerators

The curriculum of your college or university will likely include classroom-based high-impact learning experiences that are designed, in part, to help you form strong relationships with your professors and peers. A common example is a first-year seminar. Sometimes these courses are an introduction to interdisciplinary learning and exploration, other times they are classes on special topics designed to immerse students in a field of study, and still other times they focus on academic advising and serve as an extended orientation to making the most of your college experience. Often, your first-year seminar instructor may also serve as your initial academic advisor, another important relationship for you.

Another common example of a classroom-based relationship accelerator is the capstone course, a final requirement in many majors that is designed to help you integrate, synthesize, and reflect upon your learning in the discipline and perhaps also complete a semester-long project. Capstone courses also present an opportunity to celebrate an intellectual journey with your peers and faculty in your closest academic community. Some of these require you to develop and share an electronic portfolio that showcases your academic work and personal development in college. That can

▼▼▼▼▼▼▼▼▼▼▼▼▼▼▼▼▼

"I consider Professor Gavassa my mentor. I took biology from her my first semester in college. After that I asked her if I could be a learning assistant (LA) in her class. I chose to work with her because I really admired her and I saw some similar traits in her and me. I LA'd for four semesters with her. She always took that chance not only to guide me to get better at helping the students in her class as an LA, but also for me to get better for myself. She's the only teacher in college that I felt close enough to talk about some personal stuff with, and she was always there and understanding. I am really thankful for that. I'm still in contact with her to this day."

—Jennyflore Andre, Florida International University

▲▲▲▲▲▲▲▲▲▲▲▲▲▲▲▲

be a good opportunity to reconnect with professors and peers who have contributed to your success throughout college.

By talking with peers, advisors, and faculty you know, you also will be able to identify courses and professors who teach courses in ways that will have you actively learning with peers. José Robles, whom you met on the first page of this book, shows what is possible when active peer learning transforms a course that could have been "as boring as rocks." You can also take advantage of opportunities to work with learning assistants, to join online study groups, and to engage with academic topics outside the classroom by going to scholarly talks, artistic performances, and other events sponsored by your college—you might be surprised who you connect with and what ideas inspire you when you take advantage of programs and events simply because they capture your interest.

Out-of-Class Relationship Accelerators

Many forms of campus involvement—student employment, membership in clubs, and intermural or varsity athletics—can also be relationship accelerators. Chloe Inskeep of the University of Iowa is a first-generation college student who was invited to join First Gen Hawks, a program that pairs students with opportunities in leadership and engagement, undergraduate research, and on-campus employment. Chloe's on-campus job profoundly shaped her initial semester on campus:

> My employment is in the office of the vice president for student life. Every single time we see each other, the vice president talks to me about how it's going and how I'm feeling. And along with her assistant, Eric Rossow, they have been, seriously, one of the best things ever for me and my education. They make you feel like you want to be there, and they want you there.

Chloe also decided to join a club, CHAARG (Changing Health, Attitudes, and Actions to Recreate Girls), as a way to meet new friends in the midst of a pandemic:

> It's a fitness club where we work out together and have these little socials every other week in small groups, so I get to connect with a lot of people. I loved it so much I decided to become a leader. In my first year, it was hard to make connections with anyone because of the pandemic, and I decided I needed to join some clubs. I didn't go into Greek life because that's not me. So I found CHAARG and thought, "It will help me stay healthy." I made so many friends. I was not expecting to be this involved, and I love it.

"It is important for us to have a space specifically for males because the socialization process for males—particularly males of color and from certain socioeconomic statuses—does not provide spaces for us to be in community with one another in authentic ways. We are sitting side by side watching games; we are competing on a field or on a court; we are performing masculinity with one another, but we rarely have opportunities to get together and talk about how we are truly feeling and where we are going and what we are carry with us on a day-to-day basis."

—Matthew Smith, California State University, Dominguez Hills

Chloe is a good example of a student who intentionally sought out relationships, mentors, leadership opportunities, support, and friendship by fully taking advantage of the resources available to her at the University of Iowa. She took an active role in finding her relationship accelerators.

Learning Communities

The term "learning community" implies relationship building, and many colleges and universities have a variety of this type of relationship accelerator. Course-based learning communities, for instance, usually involve the same group of students taking a cluster of classes together. One advantage of this kind of learning community is that you get to know a group of peers quite well during class, without having to spend a lot (or any) time outside of the course together, which can be a barrier for many busy students.

The University of Washington has a well-known learning community program in the form of a first-year seminar. Twenty-five students in a First-Year Interest Group (FIG) take both a FIG seminar and a disciplinary course, like Introduction to Biology, together. A trained peer educator (an upper-level student) leads the FIG seminar, and all FIGs include a Projecting Forward project that requires students to interview community members from a field that interests them. For example, Max Chan, a student who hopes to work in professional sports, interviewed staff from Seattle's professional football and baseball teams—and then he shared what he learned about their work, and himself, with his peers in his FIG learning community.

Some colleges and universities also offer learning communities located in residence halls, sometimes with a faculty member mentoring or even living in an on-campus apartment as part of the community. These residential experiences typically have an academic or intellectual theme, and students might be enrolled in a core course, with common out-of-class activities (meals, discussions, films, or trivia nights) held in the residential community. In chapter 4, you met Abby Pearch, who had a powerful experience her first year in Lichty Hall, her residential learning community. As Abby's experience showed, a residential community connects students with peers and staff or faculty, often forming a strong cohort that persists long after these students no longer live together.

Whether residential or not, learning communities are an appealing and powerful relationship accelerator for many students.

▼▼▼▼▼▼▼▼▼▼▼▼▼▼▼

"I grew up overseas going to school on an American military base, with one parent who is not from the US. I thought I knew America, and then I started at the University of Iowa. That was very stressful because of how culturally different America was from what I understood as home and the people that I had surrounded myself with. My roommate became my bedrock since she was also from a multicultural background. She was raised biculturally. I was raised biculturally. And without that, I think I would have been very lost my freshman year. We had a lot of hard conversations about how culture works, and that was something that I wasn't used to talking about."

—Wren Renquist, University of Iowa

▲▲▲▲▲▲▲▲▲▲▲▲▲▲▲

Internships, Field Experiences, and Co-ops

Internships, field experiences, and cooperative work experiences (called co-ops) are opportunities to apply knowledge from your discipline or professional field in a work setting. They allow you to build relationships with working professionals who have a wealth of knowledge and experience to share, some of whom might become long-term mentors—or even employers. These experiences also help students build strong networks, gain experience on teams (more relationships!), observe both good and bad professional practices, and build resilience. Many organizations do some or part of their work remotely, including remote internships, allowing students to participate without having to physically move to the internship site—and also making it possible for students to learn important skills such as how to collaborate using digital tools.

In some majors, internships and co-ops are required for graduation. This is increasingly important today, as many companies and organizations prefer to offer entry-level, full-time employment to people who have already completed an internship, field placement, or co-op with them. Why? Because your demonstrated performance is an opportunity for hiring managers to observe many important skills, like how well you work with others, how you bounce back from mistakes, and your resilience and work ethic. In every field, these experiences are prime opportunities for you to make sure a field is a good career fit and to find some of your first professional mentors.

Your college's career services office (it might go by another name, like the internship and career placement office) has staff who can advise you about internships, field experience, and co-op placements—and many other things, too. Sometimes these offices are centralized and serve the entire institution, and other times they are based in specific schools and colleges, serving students with particular majors. Staff in these offices (as well as faculty and others at your college) can help you connect with alumni of your institution, many of whom would be delighted to take a phone call or have coffee with a current student who is seeking career advice or looking for an internship. It is never too early to begin building connections on LinkedIn and to understand that prospective internship and co-op hosts will be reviewing your social media content before making you an offer to join them.

Regrettably, some internships are unpaid, and they may be located in expensive or distant locations, adding to the cost of gaining internship experience. Many colleges offer need-based financial aid to help offset the costs of doing internships and co-ops, so ask about sources of support in your financial aid and deans' offices.

Undergraduate Research

One of the most powerful relationship accelerators is doing research under the mentorship of a faculty member. Undergraduate research gives you an opportunity to pursue a research question that fascinates you, usually over the course of a summer or multiple semesters. Students who do undergraduate research gain experience in a discipline's processes of inquiry, discovery, and creativity, and they practice professional skills like writing for and speaking with experts in their field. If you are considering graduate school in the future, there is simply no better preparation than undergraduate research. Most important of all, the relationship you form with your mentor over the course of your undergraduate research experiences will often turn out to be one of the most important of your academic career.

You might find an undergraduate research mentor by talking to experienced peers in your major and learning how they got started with their research. Or you might look over faculty bios on a departmental website and email professors to ask whether they are open to you stopping by their office hours or having a

▼▼▼▼▼▼▼▼▼▼▼▼▼▼▼▼

"My undergraduate research mentor right from the start was really careful about how I thought about science and making sure that my voice was validated and that I was asking questions in lab meetings. She also would carve out time to talk one on one about science. She'd ask what I think and really listened to what I said."

—Samantha Paskvan, University of Washington

▲▲▲▲▲▲▲▲▲▲▲▲▲▲▲▲

quick online meeting to talk about taking on an undergraduate research student (like Sam Owusu at Davidson, whom you met earlier). Most often, undergraduate research relationships begin in the classroom, as was the case for Samantha Paskvan at the University of Washington. Samantha came to UW planning for this relationship accelerator: "I kept waiting for the class or the teacher that would spark my interest so I could jump on their research project." For her, the spark appeared in a particularly engaging genetics course in which students would collaborate to solve problems. At the end of the term, she approached her professor: "I brought in my résumé, and we talked about all the different projects they were doing in the lab and also all about me. It was incredibly invigorating to talk about science, research, and life." You will find that many faculty will be receptive to talking to you about undergraduate research if you approach them with preparedness, enthusiasm, and respect.

Civic Engagement and Service Learning

Community-based learning, whether as part of a class or outside of your course work, exposes you to the people, priorities, and needs of the neighborhoods and communities that surround your institution. Civic engagement and service-learning programs will engage you with community partners (some of whom may become your mentors), expose you to both the talents and needs of community members and organizations, help you hone your professional and interpersonal skills, and teach you about the value of civic engagement in a democracy—all while you contribute to positive change in your community.

Amaya Gaines decided in her first year at Elon University to involve herself in the Village Project, a program that provides individualized tutoring in reading and mathematics for students in early grades in schools that have high proportions of students who qualify for free and reduced lunch. Amaya chose to get involved because "I believe in the power of representation and leadership of Black and Brown people in our communities." Amaya also felt compelled to put the resources of her university—including herself—to use for the good of the broader community. Her relationships with her young students and community members are important to her: "I love going to schools and meeting students and families where they are. I like being able to bond with my students over books and games we play at the end of our tutoring sessions."

Amaya's service also connects to other parts of education, including her membership in a residential learning community focused on examining social disparities, her double major in policy studies and political science, and her undergraduate research examining statewide antipoverty programs. Her service learning also supports her career goals: "Sometimes policy analysts can get distanced from the communities they are studying. Policies should not be made for communities, but *with* communities. So having community dialogue is really important, especially through first-hand experiences with people in programs like the Village Project."

Study Abroad / Study Away

In study abroad or study away, students take classes in another country or in another part of the United States. These experiences give students opportunities to see the world, build relationships in different cultural contexts, develop skills in a new language, or gain new forms of intercultural competence, such as appreciation of different worldviews and religions. Many experiences take place over the course of a full academic term, but institutions typically also offer shorter-term experiences, such as a January term or May term or during an official college break, that can be transformative and relationship rich.

Students hoping to study abroad are often concerned about (1) fitting the experience within their academic plans and personal obligations, and (2) finding scholarship aid to support additional costs, or (3) leaving the country or state for the first time and having to navigate new languages, cultures, food, and traditions. Your college's study abroad office will have a wealth of information about available programs and scholarship opportunities. Planning is key. If you aim to study abroad during your junior year, for example, your academic advisor can help you arrange your schedule so that you can still fulfill all the requirements for your degree and graduate on time. Many institutions offer special scholarship aid to help students fund the costs of a passport, airfare, and other program expenses, making this relationship accelerator more accessible to you than you might expect.

Pursue In-Depth Relationship Accelerators

Since some relationship accelerators unfold over more than one semester and require planning to make sure they align and fit within your college curriculum (such as internships and study away), early discussions with your academic advisor are important. This longer time horizon is helpful for in-depth experiential learning and building meaningful relationships. Obviously, a one-time volunteer experience on a Saturday morning is not at all the same as a semester-long service-learning course that involves having learning goals, building relationships with community partners, completing a long-term project, and reflecting on what you have learned. Relationship accelerators like these require significant time and effort, so we encourage you to pursue them in

☑ **Showcase what you've learned in relationship accelerators.** Because relationship accelerators are such an important part of your education, you should document what you have done so you can share your learning and skills with prospective employers and graduate schools. Here are some options for doing this:

- *Résumé:* Your résumé should highlight the high-impact learning you have done. Be sure your résumé features internships completed, leadership positions held, community service projects, and more. Also, remember that the relationships formed through these activities might be a good source for professional and personal references. Your college's career center can help you create your résumé, and making a connection at the career center can also help you in many other ways.
- *Electronic portfolio:* E-portfolios document student academic and creative work, along with a student's reflections on their academic, professional, and personal growth and development. For example, your e-portfolio might include an undergraduate research poster you presented at a conference, examples of work you completed during an internship, an excerpt of a group presentation you did in a course, and short statements from you explaining the significance of each of those for you. Your college's writing center can help you create an e-portfolio, and making a connection at the writing center can help you in many other ways.
- *Experiential learning transcript:* Some colleges issue both a traditional academic transcript (listing the courses you have taken, your grades, and so on) *and* an experiential learning transcript, which certifies your experience in relational accelerators like study abroad, undergraduate research, and internships. Ask your advisor about this so you know what your school provides and so you can plan to use this resource in future job or graduate school applications.

depth rather than committing yourself to too many experiences and not being able to immerse yourself in any of them.

We hope your college career will allow for many opportunities to experience how high-impact practices can help build some of the most important relationships of your life. Be bold in pursuing them—again, remember that a journey begins with a single step.

 ## Ask Yourself . . .

1. Which relationship accelerators already exist at your college? Are there any you are interested in getting involved with?

2. If you are already participating in a relationship accelerator, how is it going? Do you feel like you are connecting with faculty, staff, or peers more deeply? If so, what are you learning that you can apply to other aspects of your education and life? If not, is there anything you can do to strengthen these relationships?

Try This!

1. Search your college website to find out which relationship accelerators and high-impact practices are available to you. Use the list shown earlier in this chapter (page 95) to search for relationship accelerators individually. Choose one to learn more about, and email the person who oversees the program. If it's not listed online, ask your advisor or one of your professors where you can learn more.

2. Visit the career center at your college, and ask how you can find and apply to internships, jobs, or graduate or professional school.

3. Email a professor to ask about their research and to see if they ever involve undergraduates in their research projects.

You might contact a professor who teaches one of your favorite courses. Or you could search a department's web page to find a professor whose work interests you (as Sam Owusu did), or ask your friends if they know a professor who might be a valuable contact.

CHAPTER 8

Make the Most of Mentoring Conversations

EARLIER IN THE BOOK, you read about mentors. Logan Thomas met her mentor, Dr. Dawn Murphy, in the dean of students office during a low moment at the start of her first year at North Carolina A&T (chapter 1). Meena Alizai considers Bertha Castellanos, who leads the Empowerment Center at San Antonio College, her mentor (chapter 1). Samantha Paskvan from the University of Washington found her mentor, Professor Bonny Brewer, in her undergraduate research lab (chapter 3). Mentors are not always older or more experienced, however. Wren Renquist and Sydney Stork at the University of Iowa are not only friends, but they consider each other to be peer mentors.

Mentoring relationships like these often emerge from formal interactions (between, for example, professor and student, supervisor and employee, or coach and athlete), then they evolve over time to become more personal and reciprocal with both people contributing to and benefiting from the bond that develops. And mentoring relationships are powerful. Brad Johnson, a professor of psychology at the U.S. Naval Academy, told us:

Those of us who have mentors just do better. It doesn't matter whether you're looking at higher education, the military, or corporate America, those of us who have mentors get more opportunities. We have broader networks. We make more money. We get more promotions. We report later on that we're happier with both our careers and our lives. We tend to feel more comfortable balancing work and professional obligations. For all of these reasons, the benefits of mentoring really are not even in question anymore.

We hope you will find mentors in college, but we know the word "mentor" can feel daunting because it usually describes a formal, long-term relationship between a senior person (the mentor) and a less experienced and knowledgeable protégé (or mentee). So we are *not* simply telling you to "go find a mentor"—something you might have heard before. Instead, this chapter focuses on how you can seek out and participate in what Brad Johnson calls *mentoring conversations*. These are interactions that are not as long lasting or reciprocal as your connection to a mentor but are still significant. Sometimes they blossom into a long-term, full-fledged mentoring relationship. More often, mentoring conversations will provide you

FACT: **Mentors are guides.** "Mentor" comes from the ancient Greek drama *The Odyssey*. In the story, Mentor is an old man who acts as a moral guide to Telemachus, a young person who is uncertain and confused about how to navigate life. At crucial moments in the story, the goddess of wisdom, Athena, takes the shape of Mentor so she can advise and encourage Telemachus to make decisions that have major implications for his family and his community. That's what it means to be a mentor.

with a bit of advice, challenge, or support that you need at that time. And getting in the habit of having mentoring conversations can be like exercise—helping you develop skills and capacities that you will use over and over as you navigate college, career, and life.

College is brimming with opportunities for these kinds of discussions with faculty, staff, and peers. Mentoring conversations can happen in meetings scheduled to explore a specific topic or problem, or they might be unplanned and informal. They can be as simple as recognizing, appreciating, and affirming the talent of someone in a hallway conversation or an online exchange. They sometimes offer a challenge to do better, but with empathy and a sincere desire to help the other person grow. Usually these are small, quiet moments of connection, but occasionally they can make *a critical difference* in someone's education and life.

So how do mentoring conversations work, and how do you seek out and engage in them? In our research, we identified five things that mentoring conversations do. Understanding these five benefits will help you be alert to opportunities for moments of meaningful connection that you will encounter in college. For each, you will find ideas for seeking out—and creating—these powerful interactions.

1. Mentoring Conversations Create Space to Be Heard and to Be Human

All students need to sense that they matter to other people in college.[1] Laura Rendón, professor of higher education at the University of Texas at San Antonio, has done decades of research that shows how this validation—the feeling of being valued as a student and as a whole human—is essential for academic success and personal well-being in college, particularly for students of color and first-generation undergraduates.[2]

Mentoring conversations are one of the primary ways students—you—can experience this sense of mattering and validation. This can happen in or out of the classroom. Some colleges have staff with titles like "student success coach" who deliberately work to build this kind of relationship with all students. More often, these conversations occur spontaneously when someone reacts positively to something you say or when you really listen to someone around you. Jennyflore Andre told us about a mentoring moment she experienced at Florida International University:

> I was a resident assistant and in a meeting of all of the
> housing professionals and supervisors. We were sitting at
> a table discussing ideas for programs to put on for our
> residents. I made a comment and then went back to being
> quiet. This person—I don't even remember her name—
> walked up to me and said, "Speak up. You had a nice idea
> earlier. I know you have more ideas on your mind. Speak
> up." Those words stuck with me. At that point in time, I
> needed that.

This is one of the most important mentoring conversations for many students: assurance that their ideas matter and that their voice and perspective are significant. And it's something you can do for your peers if you are willing to offer them affirming and encouraging words.

Samer Suleman had a different kind of validating experience with a professor at the University of Iowa:

> Freshman year I took my first media course called Black
> Television Culture. There was a professor—my first
> professor—Dr. Alfred Martin, who is a Black man. I was
> like, "Oh look. It's me." I went to his office hours and

remember him getting real with me for a moment. He told me he really does his best to make his Black male students feel like they are being prioritized and that they are working to their potential. And that he would be there to support them. I thought that was nice to hear. I felt like, okay, Dr. Martin is somebody I can reach out to, because he extended that invitation.

Discovering that his first professor in college shared his racial identity was important and reassuring to Samer, especially on a predominantly White campus like Iowa. Notice, too, that Samer took the initiative to go to Professor Martin's office to introduce himself. By doing that, Samer made this mentoring conversation possible. Professor Martin's invitation to visit his office at any time, his gift of a candid conversation, and his offer of future guidance is a perfect combination of the academic, emotional, and well-being support that can result from a mentoring conversation—and that can develop into a long-term mentoring relationship.

You can help create space to be heard and to be human by taking small steps like visiting a faculty member's office hours, introducing yourself to a peer in class or in a dining hall, engaging seriously in a breakout room discussion during an online course, or stopping by a campus office that looks interesting to you. And remember, simple questions like "How are you?" can be a good way to start a conversation that might, or might not, turn into a deeper discussion.

▼▼▼▼▼▼▼▼▼▼▼▼▼▼▼▼

"The person who makes the biggest difference for our online students is likely to be their advisor or writing coach because they are the ones who can provide that sustained relationship. If I am your coach, I tend to know what is going on in your world. I have come to know about your family. I have a sense of what your struggles are at school, and I am the one you are most likely to call when you run into a snafu."

—President Paul LeBlanc,
Southern New Hampshire University

▲▲▲▲▲▲▲▲▲▲▲▲▲▲▲▲

2. Mentoring Conversations Can Provide Practical Guidance and Knowledge

College can be filled with unfamiliar terminology and expectations. One of the important purposes of mentoring conversations is to provide practical knowledge and guidance that will allow students to successfully navigate the sometimes bumpy terrain of college—what's expected of you, how to take advantage of all the resources that are available to you, and why you should keep asking questions about anything you do not understand. This practical guidance not only helps you be successful academically, but it also can be important for your personal well-being.

Moon Medina, a student at Florida International University, recalls an essential conversation with a graduate teaching assistant encouraging them—already a good student—to raise their expectations for the quality of their academic work and giving them practical advice about how to study more effectively in political science:

> I would consider my TA for international relations in my first year—the first class in my major—a mentor of the moment. She really helped get me into the mindset of "OK, I'm a college student now." I realized there was a different level of expectation for me in this class. It was probably the first class I have ever gotten a B in in my life. So that was a very good reality check when she told me, "You are doing great work, but I really need you to click in—to click out of high school and into college. This is college."

Mentoring conversations also open students' perspectives about taking advantage of campus opportunities and resources. Meena Alizai at San Antonio College (you read about her in chapter 1) had a friend, Julia, who admired her good grades. One day, Julia asked Meena what she did when she was not in class. That quickly turned into a conversation about getting a campus job, something Julia had done but Meena didn't even know was possible: "So I applied, and after a week I started working in the campus library. It was good advice. I was studying, I was working and gaining experience, and financially it was helping me."

When you are a new student or after you transfer to a different school, you likely will be the one seeking knowledge and advice. Don't be shy about asking professors, staff, and peers for guidance. They can help! As you gain more experience on your way toward graduation, you will be the one who can share practical guidance and information with other students, whether you are in a formal peer-mentoring role or you are just chatting informally online or in person. A friendly smile and a bit of practical wisdom can make a big difference in helping students (including you) feeling like they matter and can be successful in college.

3. Mentoring Conversations Might Provide a "Warm Handoff" to Another Person

Few people have the capacity to advise and support someone in every dimension of their lives. Sometimes a mentoring conversation should connect a person with a counselor, advisor, professor, or friend—a person with the expertise or knowledge that is needed in that situation. A "warm handoff" is a simple and personalized way to introduce someone to new connections and thus broaden their networks. For example, rather than simply saying to a peer, "Maybe you could speak to someone at the counseling center," you might make that suggestion feel less intimidating by sharing a story about when you benefited from counseling, or by pointing out specific resources and programs on the college website, or by sitting with them as they email or call to make an appointment, or even by offering to walk your friend to an initial visit.

Mirella Cisneros Perez did not feel at home for her first three semesters at Elon University. Fortunately, some students she met through a peer-mentoring program offered her a warm handoff:

> My peers led me to the Latinx Hispanic Union. Once I was a part of that organization, my experience at Elon shifted completely. I felt like I belonged somewhere, and I had people I could go to and connect with. This ultimately led me to meeting Dean Sylvia Muñoz and other people in the Center for Race, Ethnicity, and Diversity Education who I looked up to. Whenever I would run into them, I knew that they believed in me and wanted me to succeed. The connections my peers guided me to helped me find my place at Elon and changed my whole experience at Elon for the positive.

That introduction helped Mirella feel validated, find community, get a campus job, and establish a relationship with someone who has become a lifelong mentor. Today Mirella is the community impact manager for LatinxEd, a nonprofit investing in Latinx leadership and expanding educational equity and opportunity in North Carolina—she is dedicating her career to having the kinds of mentoring conversations that transformed her own education.

A warm handoff often involves making a personal introduction, which minimizes the chance the hoped-for connection will fall through the cracks. Kindness and graciousness help make this happen for you and for your peers. With a warm handoff, one mentoring conversation creates even more relationships. Don't hesitate to ask someone to make an introduction for you ("I know you do research with Professor Zang. Would you mind introducing me to her sometime? I'd like to learn more about her research."). When you become more experienced, look for opportunities to connect your peers with faculty, staff, or other students you know. Sometimes a simple step like a text ("In class we talked about the debate club. I'm going to the club meeting tonight. Do you want to go with me?") can lead to a warm handoff that will transform a student's time in college.

4. Mentoring Conversations Help during Low Moments in Life

College can be hard—failing a test or a course, losing a friend, struggling to make enough money to pay the bills while you care for yourself and your family, and so much more. Most students encounter such difficulties at some point in college, and many face significant challenges throughout their time in school. Mentoring conversations can go a long way toward helping you either get back on track or adjust to your next situation.

Aigné Taylor is a political science and sociology double major at North Carolina A&T. She recalls her arrival on campus:

> I came to A&T a very insecure young Black girl. Growing up, I always felt like an outcast because I was always the one Black girl on the cheer team or the Black girl in the AP course or the Black girl who was interested in politics. Coming to A&T, it was okay for me to wear my hair natural, it was okay to be loud, and it was okay for me to be myself authentically. But it was a long journey for me to get that way.

Professor Antja Caldwell noticed the insecurities that Aigné was working so hard to hide. She invited Aigné to stop by her office sometime. When she did, Professor Caldwell told her, "You're a great student, but I see you hold back sometimes in class discussions." Then she handed Aigné a mirror.

> She had this mirror on her desk, and she was like, "Look at yourself." And at the time it was very hard for me to just look in the mirror and go, "Okay, this is Aigné Taylor, and this is who I am." I said, "I really don't want to look in the mirror," but I finally looked in the mirror, and I actually teared up a little bit. I realized how really insecure I am. And I don't have to be that way.

Professor Caldwell recommended that Aigné listen to the song "Unpretty" by TLC, which Aigné says she did every single day throughout college. "She doesn't realize how much of an impact she had on me. I'm not sure she even remembers her telling me that, but it really had a huge impact on me because anytime I feel insecure, I remember what she told me: 'Aigné, you can do this.'"

This mentoring conversation had a life-changing impact on Aigné because Professor Caldwell identified a significant problem, approached it directly but with sensitivity and skill, and then offered a specific strategy to help Aigné. Not everyone can do that, but you should be looking for opportunities to lift up a peer who is having a hard time or to connect with someone when you are struggling. College counseling and advising offices can be a good place to start if you are not sure who to talk with about a challenge you are facing. If you notice a peer who seems to be

"I was scared to look my teachers in the eye when I hadn't been there for three weeks, and it was only an eleven-week class. That was tough. But they were willing to help me dig myself out of that hole. I learned not to be scared of messing up, but to be scared of letting my fear get in the way of the life that I want for myself."

—Nellie Bourne, San Antonio College

stressed or in trouble, even asking "How are you doing?" can create an opportunity for them to talk with you, if they are willing and able to do so. Remember, you do not have to solve their problems or become their therapist, but you can connect them with college resources—and make a warm handoff to be sure they feel supported along the way.

5. Mentoring Conversations Will Leave Legacies

Although mentoring conversations in college are often brief, they can have long-lasting impacts. At times you may talk with people who inspire you with their intelligence, grace, or passion, sparking you to think "I want to be like them!"

Sydney Stork, a biology major at the University of Iowa, caught a glimpse of her future self when she was impressed by the leadership abilities of one of her peers:

> When I was taking organic chemistry there was an SI [supplemental instructor] leader for that course who was a mentor of the moment for me. I just really liked her leading style, and she was very compassionate and empathetic too. It's a fairly challenging course, and she understood that and did what she could to help students in a great way. It was the best course I took in college, mostly because of the SI experience I had there. And she also really inspired me to eventually become the SI leader for organic chemistry—just because I really liked the way she interacted with the material and with students. I don't keep up closely with her anymore—I follow her on Instagram—but that was an impactful relationship.

While Sydney's mentoring conversations took place over the course of the semester in a peer-to-peer instructional capacity, her SI did much more than help her with organic chemistry; she served as a role model and an inspiration for Sydney, encouraging her to become an SI, where she could have the same effect on other students in organic chemistry.

Matt Foster, an engineering major and football player at Elon University, graduated as team captain and Colonial Athletic Association student-athlete of the year. But at the end of his first year, he felt like he desperately needed advice and direction:

> I was looking for a summer internship and had no idea where to go, where to apply, or who would be a connection for me. So I asked Cayce Crenshaw, the assistant athletics director for academic support who is a built-in mentor and helps keep all the student athletes on the straight and narrow, "What am I supposed to do this summer?" And she set me up with the Summer Undergraduate Research Experience program. I ended up working with engineering professor Dr. Blackmon and really enjoyed doing research with him. At the end of the summer, I asked him, "Where can I go from here, and how can I keep doing this?" He connected me to Dr. Walter and Dr. Su, and I started doing research with them. Eventually, this led to creating a start-up company and to having connections with the entrepreneurship center on campus. All of those things happened because of me asking Casey, "Hey, what am I going to do this summer?"

Matt's question to the right person at the right moment influenced his college career and life in a significant way, leaving a long-term legacy from a brief and casual mentoring conversation.

You Can Make Mentoring Conversations Happen

You can increase your chances of having mentoring conversations by taking small steps, like the students we quote in this chapter: stay after class to talk with your professor; ask questions of college staff; schedule coffee or an online chat with a student who is a year or two ahead of you in your major; keep your ears open for words of praise, support, and challenge, and then act upon them; join a club or organization where you will find people with similar interests, identities, and passions; form a study group for one of your classes. You don't need to connect with everyone you meet, but the more you offer a welcoming word and a listening ear, the more likely your college experiences will be defined by rich mentoring conversations.

Many students also do not realize that they are not only on the receiving end of these exchanges. Often, you can act as a "mentor of the moment" for a peer by initiating a meaningful conversation. That requires you to be aware of the needs of the people around you, to show genuine interest in and openness with others, and to be willing to take the risk of asking for or offering kindness, guidance, or generous listening. This doesn't have to be complicated. In our interviews, many students commented on the power of someone simply caring enough to pause and genuinely ask, "How are you?"

Mentors and mentoring conversations will help you build a bridge from your education to what comes after college: connecting to a job or graduate school and helping you think about the impact you want to have on the world as an engaged citizen. The next chapter will help you think about how your mentoring conversations can become part of a larger whole—a constellation of relationships.

Ask Yourself . . .

1. Can you think of a moment when someone's comment or action moved you from feeling at the margins to a place of belonging? Could you make a comment or take an action that would do this for one of your peers?
2. Describe a time when someone passed off some essential knowledge to you to aid in your adjustment to college. Have you done this for others?
3. When in your life has someone led you to someone or something that made a critical difference? How did they do it?
4. Describe a mentoring conversation when someone has helped you through a low moment.
5. Has a mentoring conversation ever left a legacy for you? How so?

 # Try This!

1. Choose one of your professors, whether from a class you're currently taking or one you took in another term, and reach out to request a meeting (see sample email at the end of chapter 5). Bring a couple of questions with you, questions that are not easily answered with a yes or no. You might ask about the professor's career or for advice on how to be a successful college student.
2. Practice having a mentoring conversation with one of your peers. Ask "How are you?" or "What's your favorite class right now? Why?" or "What's the hardest part of this semester for you?" and take the time to listen.

CHAPTER 9

Building Your Relationship Constellation

WHILE THE LAST CHAPTER zoomed in on individual mentors and mentoring conversations, this chapter zooms out and invites you to picture the total web of your relationships—what we call your *constellation of relationships and mentors*. Sydney Stork, a student at the University of Iowa, describes the idea of a constellation like this:

> If I compartmentalize my life in college, I've had two separate jobs, plus research, and I've worked in my department on diversity and inclusion issues. For each of these areas, I've had at least one significant person, and they all fulfilled a different role for me. So I do think it's important to have a constellation, because you can't rely on one group or one person for all your needs or to help get you to where you want to go or to help you in your struggles.

As Sydney points out, one of the main reasons you want to work toward having a constellation of relationships while in college is that you are a multidimensional person. And as a college student, you will develop a variety of academic and personal interests. The idea of a constellation means that instead of trying to find one person or a small group of people to support your multiple interests and needs, you can cultivate a whole web of relationships to enrich your life in—and after—college.

Developing this constellation is one of the most significant parts of your college experience, particularly if you create it intentionally over time. This chapter will share how several college students built their constellations and guide you through a process of building your own network of relationships during your college years.

Types of Constellations and Purposeful Connections

The image and idea of a constellation come from Brad Johnson, the psychology professor you met in chapter 8. Johnson explains that most people do not have just one mentor. Instead, successful and happy people tend to have "a constellation of mentors," which he defines as "the set of relationships an individual has with people who take an active interest in and action to advance the individual's career by assisting with his or her personal and professional development."[1] In other words, anyone who actively supports you—whether as a student or as a person—is in your constellation.

Imagine that you are a star in the night sky and that you are connected to many other stars who might represent your most important professors and teachers; people with whom you share intellectual passions; peers who "show you the ropes" about succeeding in college; individuals who represent your personal and emotional support system and affirm your identities; a person who inspired you to go to college in the first place or to consider a career in a specific profession; the coach of your athletic team; your job and internship supervisors; a religious or spiritual leader in your life; and the friends with whom you are comfortable sharing your daily laughter and tears. These people, both individually and collectively, make up your constellation—and they will be important to you as you navigate college, develop in your career, and pursue your goals for a meaningful and purposeful life.

It may be helpful to think about your constellation or web of relationships in terms of categories that describe the roles individuals will play in your life. Some relationships will be mostly *academic* or *intellectual*; they make you excited about learning or help you develop new skills. Other connections will support your *emotional or spiritual belonging*, your *well-being*, or your sense that you *matter*. A third set of individuals may play a more *practical* role—showing you how to navigate college or introducing you to an organization or job. Finally, others may have a longer-term impact, helping you *become an engaged citizen of the world*.

In terms of what your constellation looks like, there's no formula or perfect shape. Some people have constellations or networks that are tightly connected—everybody knows everybody. Other people have constellations that look more like octopuses—a set of people over here and a different set of people over there, and they don't know each other.[2] Dylan Costo from Florida International University (FIU) told us that both in high school and in college, he intentionally looked for relationships that were not connected to one another:

> Let's say that you have a tight network of friends and
> professors. You can consider that our solar system,
> because the planets are close to each other and to other
> stars. And you can learn a lot from that particular system.
> But in my experience, I was never a part of one group. I
> would always jump around to different groups because

I can learn something different from them. So instead of staying in one solar system, I would go and try to find other systems and see if I can learn something from them. They're not connected. They don't share the same qualities, but you can learn a lot from the different systems, the different sets of friends. And that was my experience in college as well.

Dylan's fellow FIU student Moon Medina told us that the individual relationships in their constellation may have differed, but "in the end, they all converge on different aspects of my own identity." From a best friend and roommate to co-workers and mentors, in Moon's case, "we all have a similar goal. We all have some similar mindsets." Moon also found it important to try to deepen their relationships by asking individuals from their constellation to engage in other aspects of their life, like asking a co-worker to participate in a social activity: "That's when you really learn more about them and move from being just an acquaintance to being a mentor or a friend."

Who Could Be in Your Constellation?

If there's someone in your life you consider a mentor, this person would indeed be an important star in your constellation. But not all important and meaningful relationships in colleges are necessarily this intense, formal, or high stakes. Yet they can still become part of your constellation. For example:

- A student officer in a club you belong to can teach you a great deal about leadership and running organizations.
- The professor who takes the time to give you encouraging feedback on your assignments might recognize talents in you.

- A librarian can greet you warmly each time you use a library study space or help you make sure you're using credible sources in your research.
- If you are a student-athlete, your coach can help you build resilience and confidence, as well as higher levels of athleticism.
- A campus job supervisor can help you learn about professional skills that are critical in the workplace environment.
- A person who shares an important identity with you, such as race, religion, or gender identity, might be a key role model, supporter, and friend.
- The supervisor of your summer internship might be a critical link to full-time employment following graduation.
- A counselor or therapist might be a crucial person in your life to maintain good mental health.
- A priest, imam, rabbi, minister, or other spiritual leader might be someone to whom you turn for guidance.
- The TA you had for chemistry lab might turn out to be a good resource for learning about the process of applying to graduate school.
- Your group of close friends likely demonstrate many qualities of good character that you would like to emulate.
- A close extended family member, like an older cousin that comes to visit you in college or calls you to check in, may provide some comfort from home and serve as

"When I look back on my college experiences, the only things I regret are not doing things sooner and not doing more or being afraid of talking to one person or going to office hours or making any connection, however, big or small."

—Sydney Stork, University of Iowa

a source of motivation when you are going through a tough time.

When you stop to think about it, you likely already have some stars in your constellation.

The Value of a Diverse Constellation

Brad Johnson's research demonstrates that "a mentoring constellation will be strongest and most effective when the [student] is intentional about forming the constellation and when the constellation contains good diversity." In the previous chapters, we discussed one kind of relationship diversity by encouraging you to connect to not only your peers, but also your professors and the many individuals who work at your college. Here, we focus on differences in gender, race, socioeconomic class, intellectual viewpoint, and language. If the great problems of the twenty-first century are to be resolved—if we are to reduce inequities in health, wealth, education, and opportunity based on race and ethnicity; respond to climate change; strengthen democracy—citizens and leaders will need to work across these categories of differences more than any previous generation. Your college experience is a unique chance for you to encounter diversity both in and out of the classroom, allowing you to critically examine your values and to develop the professional, civic, and personal capacities that will enable you to make a positive contribution to your community and the world.

One of the most effective ways to prepare to thrive in your future is to intentionally seek difference in your constellation of relationships. This usually requires getting uncomfortable and learning new skills. If everyone in your constellation shares the same political viewpoints or personal characteristics (such as age, race, gender and gender identity, nationality, abilities, religion, and economic class), you are missing an opportunity to have your perspectives and sense of the world enlarged, your mindset challenged, and your friendship circles enlivened. Keep this in mind as you seek relationships that will challenge you, expose you to new perspectives, help you understand that you have a lot of new things to learn—and perhaps to unlearn. College is an opportunity for you to stretch and grow.

Straightforward Strategies for Beginning and Growing Your Constellation

START SIMPLE AND SMALL

Recall Ruth Moreno, a student at San Antonio College, who was fortunate to meet two people at the beginning of her college career who were her earliest advocates and guides. In Ruth's words, "My constellation radiates from those two people." Jim Lucchelli and Bertha Castellanos became essential champions for Ruth's success. As chapter 1 described, it only takes one or two key relationships in college to begin your constellation. For specific steps you might take to connect with your peers, professors, or staff members at your college, revisit the "Try This" ideas at the end of chapters 4, 5, and 6.

BE AWAKE FOR "TAP ON THE SHOULDER" MOMENTS

In your college career, potential mentors might say things to you like, "You have a talent for this subject" or "I see you really have a heart for community service" or "I admire the leadership you just showed." These are moments when someone is holding up a mirror to you to help you gain self-understanding, just as Aigné Taylor experienced at North Carolina A&T (chapter 8). Do not brush those moments aside. Reflect on what the person has just told you and what you have just learned about yourself, and think about whether this is the start of an important conversation that might lead to something more significant.

SEEK ADVICE, FEEDBACK, AND HONESTY

Most people begin by placing another person in their constellation because they have shown themselves to be a strong source of support. But many other kinds of relationships will provide expertise that you need as well. The scholar Priscilla Claman emphasizes that many of the people in your constellation "should know more than you about something, be better than you about something, or offer different points of view. Putting only buddies [in your constellation] won't help you grow and develop."[3] In this spirit, welcome feedback and listen carefully to honest, constructive advice, even if it might be challenging to hear. Karey Frink from Hope College did that with Professor Peaslee, her "wizard" chemistry teacher who helped her discover her passion outside of the lab (chapter 5). You will soon come to appreciate that honest feedback is truly a gift.

NURTURE RELATIONSHIPS

Relationships require attention and care, and they naturally evolve over time. You do not need to check in with everyone in your constellation on a weekly basis, but occasional updates, emails, texts, or coffee dates remind people in your constellation that you value them, that you want them to know what is happening in your life, and that you care about them as well. Asma Shauib did this when she would stop in to chat with her first professors at LaGuardia Community College, and they always reminded her to believe in herself—an important message for each of us to hear regularly. You might also act on an instinct to build a deeper relationship with someone who engaged you in an important mentoring conversation so that person becomes a part of your constellation.

As you remain connected, you may notice your relationships shifting over time; Dylan Costo found that after four years of office-hour conversations with Professor Rodriguez, he began to think of his former professor as his friend. Other important relationships may be designed to last for a fixed period of time, like a summer internship supervisor or your mentor on a semester-long community service project. It is wise to keep these important people in your network, even if you no longer speak often.

Prepare to Be a Star in the Constellations of Others

The primary emphasis of this chapter has been on forming your own relationship constellation. But you will also become a mentor to others, especially your peers. When someone approaches you for help—or when you notice someone who could use a word of encouragement or some practical advice—that is the time to pay forward the same generosity, kindness, welcome, and counsel that was shown to you. This can be as simple as introducing yourself, asking someone how they're doing, or sharing your story—whether it's how you overcame challenges, what resources at your college have been most helpful to you, or who your favorite professors have been.

When you reflect on what was most meaningful to you in college—five, ten, or fifteen years after your graduation—what will matter to you most will be the people who helped shape your life during these important years. One of the most meaningful roles you can play throughout your life is to mentor and nurture other human beings, and your college experience is an extraordinary opportunity to practice this art.

Ask Yourself . . .

1. How would you describe your current constellation or web of relationships?
2. What do you want your constellation to become?
3. Comparing your current constellation to the one you want to have, what's missing? What's one thing you could do now to help develop the constellation you'd like to have?

Try This!

Danielle Lake, director of Design Thinking at Elon University, created an exercise to help students reflect on a series of questions about four domains of relationships in college: academic/intellectual, emotional/belonging/spiritual/well-being, practical, and becoming an engaged citizen. You will find the full exercise on the book's website (ConnectionsAreEverything.org). For now, take a few minutes to reflect on the people in your life who are (or who could become) part of your constellation in each of these areas. These questions will help you identify them:

ACADEMIC/INTELLECTUAL

1. Which faculty member, peer, or staff member has made you excited about learning, challenged you, and actively engaged you in the learning process?
2. Which faculty member, peer, or staff member has left you feeling inspired, and for what reason?
3. Has a faculty member or supervisor commented on something that you are good at or on work that you have done that shows good potential?

4. Which faculty members do you feel drawn to talk to outside of class?

EMOTIONAL/BELONGING/SPIRITUAL/WELL-BEING

1. Which peers on campus do you most admire and have qualities you want to emulate? How would you describe them (friend, peer mentor, etc.)?
2. Are there staff members on campus that have been champions of your success?
3. Who do you turn to when you need emotional support?
4. Do you have a person in your life that you talk to about values that ground you?
5. Who in your constellation of relationships shares an important identity with you?

PRACTICAL

1. Which people on campus (or elsewhere) have helped you find direction in college?
2. Is there a key individual who has helped you to feel at home on campus and extended a special sense of welcome?
3. If you work on or off campus, is there an individual in your work environment that you consider a mentor, teacher, or confidant?
4. Which peers have helped you develop knowledge and confidence about negotiating the college experience, including academics, clubs and organizations, and social life?

BECOMING AN ENGAGED CITIZEN

1. Who do you talk to about how you can make a difference in your community?
2. Who is a role model for you in terms of being a leader in your community?
3. Who helps you see big issues from a global perspective?

4. Who understands your talents and interests and can help you think about what you want to do with your life after college?

5. Who might be best positioned to help you explore a specific career, perhaps through an internship or field experience?

Conclusion

Take These Ideas with You

YOUR COLLEGE IS FULL OF PEOPLE and programs designed to support and challenge you as a student. You are not on your own. You are surrounded by resources that can and should contribute to your academic success and your personal well-being in college. Connecting with people and programs will help you learn, thrive, and succeed.

We close by synthesizing six overarching ideas about relationship-rich education, and then we share wise advice from four of the students we interviewed. They have been in your shoes, and they have powerful advice to offer. On the book's website (ConnectionsAreEverything.org), you will find a variety of resources and activities to guide you through the process of preparing to make your college education relationship rich. We hope you will work through some of those online activities with someone you trust: a professor, advisor, peer, or family member.

Six Things to Know about Relationship-Rich Education

1. **Relationships will help you succeed in college.** The time and effort you spend establishing and nourishing relationships will help you persist through the challenges of college and increase the value of your college experience. Research on higher education clearly shows that the quality of relationships students form with peers, faculty, and staff is closely linked to the quality of experiences students have, including how much they learn, how likely they are to graduate, and whether they feel they belong and matter in college. Relationships will enable you to succeed academically and to thrive personally in college.

2. **Relationships will make your college experience more meaningful.** College is a time to ask big questions: Who am I and who am I becoming? What are my talents and passions? What contributions do I want to make to the world? What do I want to do in service to others? These questions, and others like them, are best explored in conversation with people who know you well. The peers, faculty, and staff who both support and challenge you in college will help you critically explore these big questions. Sometimes they will see your potential and passions more clearly than you do yourself. These kinds of meaningful interactions can transform your college experience from the pursuit of a degree into a life-changing opportunity for growth.

3. **The relationships you form in college will matter long after you graduate.** The time and effort you spend establishing and nourishing relationships in college will contribute to your professional and personal well-being years after college. Research shows that graduates who had mentoring relationships while in college report thriving in their careers and lives more than their peers who did not. Students who have meaningful rela-

tionships with faculty and staff may also discover that some of these connections last for decades, and your deepest peer connections may become friends for life. Maya Angelou is often credited with saying "people will never forget how you made them feel." Even if you do not maintain lifelong ties with everyone in college, you will always remember the ways these people made you feel valued, smart, included, capable, and hopeful.

4. **Relationship building in college prepares you to work and live in a diverse world.** The relationships you form in college offer you a unique opportunity to prepare for working and living in our complex world. Higher education institutions bring together people from varied backgrounds and cultures, immersing them in an environment that is ripe with possibilities to learn about identities, beliefs, viewpoints, and other important dimensions of humanity. The relationships you develop with peers, faculty, and staff who are different from you will help you understand and formulate your own values and will encourage you to appreciate the perspectives and lived experiences of others. By doing that, the opportunities you take to interact with and across differences in college will prepare you to exercise the leadership and citizenship that will be required to meet the great challenges ahead, including strengthening our democratic society, seeking peace, and restoring the health of the planet.

5. **You will both benefit from and contribute to relationships in college.** Relationship building is a virtuous cycle, one in which you will give and receive simultaneously. Of course, you can and should reach out to people when you need help, but you shouldn't connect with others only when you need assistance. Remember that you have a lot to offer too. By intentionally reaching out to support, guide, and mentor your peers, you can positively influence the experiences of many other students. The skills and capacities you develop by doing that in college

will empower you to contribute to positive change in organizations and communities after you graduate.

6. **You have what it takes to build relationships in college**. Your first year in college, or after you transfer to a new institution, can be particularly important in establishing meaningful connections with peers, faculty, and staff. Don't wait to get started! At the same time, don't worry if you have not found your people yet. Keep taking small steps, and you *will* build significant relationships. You don't need hundreds of connections. One or two can be transformational. Also regularly remind yourself of your strengths and values, and remember that you have made connections before; you can absolutely do this.

The knowledge, skills, and relationships you cultivate in college will matter throughout your life. The more you take advantage of the many opportunities available in college, the more successful and the happier you will be after you graduate. And it's not all about you. The world needs more citizens, neighbors, employers, co-workers, friends, spouses, parents—more people—who recognize the value of human relationships and who build meaningful connections with others, particularly people who are different from them.

Student Words of Wisdom

In our interviews, we heard from smart and thoughtful students—people just like you. Because their voices and perspectives have profoundly shaped our thinking and writing, we want to showcase their wisdom as we conclude the book.

1. **Strive to know yourself**. When we interviewed North Carolina A&T student Brandon Daye, he said that the foundation of every student's time in college is clear:

You have to find yourself. You can't show up in spaces, you can't become a leader, if you don't know yourself. Because it's not genuine, it's not authentic, it's not true. If you don't know yourself, you can't help others. Everybody's not going to know their whole self, but developing your true self to where you can just be so much better for every person you meet. What are you doing each day to become an agent of change, to better yourself, to awaken your full potential?

Brandon went on to tell us that the best way to find yourself, "to awaken your full potential," is to spend time in college with peers, faculty, and staff who will challenge you to grow and to be true to your values.

2. **Use the resources at your college**. San Antonio College graduate Nellie Bourne advises, "Use the resources available to you. No one can help you unless you let them." Drawing on and connecting with the many people and resources at your college who are there to support students is a sign of strength and a personal sense of agency—being in charge of your own destiny. Nellie insists that "no one can *stop* you unless you let them." The resources of your college, from inspiring faculty and compassionate staff to an array of student support offices to peer mentors, are there for you. Use them.

3. **Challenge your doubts**. Sydney Stork, from the University of Iowa, says she knows it's not easy to ask for help or believe in yourself. Every college student has doubts. Still, Sydney told us:

> Challenge every anxiety that you have. I feel every time I look back on my experiences, the only things I regret are not doing things sooner and not doing more or being afraid of talking to one person or going to office hours or making any connection, however big or small. So, it's a time full of anxieties, but challenge each and every one.

That's good advice, even though it can feel hard to do. Talking with a trusted peer—or a professor or advisor—at your college might be the crucial first step you need to work through your fears.

4. **Don't do college alone.** Logan Thomas, a mechanical engineering student at North Carolina A&T, told us about a strategy that worked for her and that research suggests works for most students—don't go through college alone. When we asked her what she does as a student peer mentor at A&T, Logan said, "We take them with us. I have all these tips, all this knowledge. I'm not going to let other students sit around and fail their classes." Logan realizes that there are consequences when students don't form relationships or have peer support. We find great inspiration in Logan's summary of her overall philosophy about being a mentor to peers: "We have a very close connection, and I really love mentoring them and guiding them, making them as great as they can be—even better than me. I try to pass on the passion."

We are certain if you know yourself like Brandon, seek help from the people and resources at your college like Nellie, challenge every doubt like Sydney, and do college with others like Logan, you too will have a successful, meaningful, and rewarding college journey.

College is rarely easy, but we are confident—based on our research and our decades working with students like you—that you are capable of thriving academically and personally. The peers, faculty, and staff you connect with will make your time in college more meaningful and joyful and will prepare you to flourish professionally and personally after you graduate. Small steps can take you on a long journey. Start today.

You can do this!

Afterword

TIMOTHY K. EATMAN AND MOHAMED A. FARGE

Rutgers University–Newark

In learning you will teach, and in teaching you will learn.

—Phil Collins

WE BELIEVE that the notion of relationship-rich education is self-evident. Does any real education take place outside of relationships? We think not. Student and professor, mentor and mentee, we find ourselves blessed to be linked powerfully together, with higher education as the connector. Indeed, college brought us together. But what does that really mean? How did we—the authors of this afterword—get here? Is a relationship like ours an atypical, unusual, or even plausible feature of the college experience for many students?

While gains from traditional mentoring relationships are well documented and impressive, this book takes a much more expansive view of mentoring—the relationship-rich variety. The opportunity to co-write the afterword of this important book invites us—Timothy K. Eatman, inaugural dean of the Honors Living-Learning Community (HLLC), and Mohamed A. Farge, HLLC Scholar—to reflect on our journey to provide a culminating example of the kind of relationship-rich education detailed in the book.

At the outset, it is important to note that while we are very fond of each other and enjoy a deep bond, many differences characterize our relationship. For example, we are clearly from different generations. Dean Eatman has never played PlayStation 5 (although Mohamed says he will teach him). HLLC Scholar Farge was raised in the internet era and finds PS5 second nature. We are both men of faith but practice different faiths and respect the range. Further, we are intellectually grounded in different disciplines: sociology and business. In fact, we often observe that these differences strengthen our relationship while providing interesting nuance to our interactions. Neither our similarities nor our differences, however, have ever served as a litmus test in the unfolding of our relationship.

True maximization of any relationship comes with reciprocation of both effort and consistency. These principles operate within higher education in the same ways they do in the larger society. In their 2020 book *Relationship-Rich Education*,[1] coauthors Peter Felten and Leo Lambert articulated the critical role that faculty and staff play in developing relationship-rich education. And while that book is geared toward higher-education professionals, students also have a responsibility to take ownership in establishing and nurturing such relationships—which is the focus of the book you have just read.

The balance of this afterword employs a dialogic design, providing a peek into our world. We acknowledge that our approach may be unorthodox but hope that it serves to punctuate the principles upon which the book rests.

> MOHAMED FARGE
> Hey Dean, wanted to check in on your well-being. Not hearing back from you has me a bit uneasy, please reach out when you can

TIMOTHY EATMAN

Scholar son, I am so glad that we have the opportunity to co-author this afterword but want to begin with an apology. When I saw your text two days ago, I did not want to rush a response, got caught up and getting back to you in a timely manner slipped through the cracks of my schedule. Seeing the care in your message reminded me of how fortunate I am to be connected with you and that I don't ever want you to think that I am taking you for granted. While it may be a bit embarrassing for me, I am glad that you agreed to use the text message in this afterword. I think it gives a window into our rich relationship.

MF

No worries, I was just a bit concerned. Once you told me about this opportunity, I've been waiting to think through it together, but besides that I just wanted to make sure you were ok given I hadn't heard back in a bit.

TE

Means a lot, son. Listen I wonder if you have a story to share that gives a window into our relationship. Like what would you say made you take me seriously about my offer to encourage and support the Scholars in your HLLC cohort; many did not take advantage of the opportunity and I always wonder what makes the difference.

MF

I think it was less about what you did or said and more about how I received it, or how long it took me to internalize the message in general. From the onset of my time at Rutgers, you were adamant in being there for your students, me included, but really it was when I was at a time of need that I felt a push to accepting your invitation. And that push is something

I believe many students experience, particularly during their first few years in a new environment.

How do you feel about that? The fact that students oftentimes seek support when they need it versus embracing your offering of serious support, which you try to provide for all of your students, from the beginning of their journey, before a problem arises.

TE

It makes sense to me that need is often the catalyst. I told you about my college mentor Dr. George Mims who at 88 years old is still very much in my life. Dr. Mims had a way of communicating that we should take seriously his offers of support. Far too many students do not have support at the beginning of the journey; however, I'm always struck by the decision point at which those who do have such access become activated and engaged.

It is a real delight to read the manuscript with you and I am really impressed, but not surprised by your thoughts, reactions and analyses. Care to share some as we conclude.

MF

Sure, Dean. As previously mentioned, with any rich relationship there is a significant amount of reciprocal servicing for relationships to thrive. I see this in our relationship. And this all started with your help from when I entered Rutgers. In chapter 3, the authors mention scholars finding "what students do in college is far more important than the type of institution they attend." As you know, this sentiment was one I needed to internalize upon entering Rutgers–Newark, especially after making the decision to not go to my dream school (Howard University). It was then that I began to see the opportunity of the institution I was in, the opportunity to meet the many great people at Rutgers–Newark, you included. With you always expressing your accessibility I knew that this was an environment that I could appreciate. And even though I was initially hesitant to your invitation, I think it is useful for readers to know that within the semester I found myself emboldened enough to notify you that I was your new intern for my remaining years at Rutgers University. I liken the experience to caretaking, and the contrast between preventative care and curative care. If students initially understand that not accepting the invitation of mentorship and guidance, particularly from leaders in higher education like you, they are doing a disservice to their journey because not only can there be hardships in their higher education career; there will be. And when those valleys appear, it is difficult to seek help when already flustered as opposed to already having advocates excited to support you.

TE

You sure did declare, "I am your intern" and I remember afresh the sense of bold animation that you presented. It was not clear at first how serious you were, and I did not have any mentoring plan. My heart is full when students take me seriously. The epigraph you chose for this afterword speaks to the deep reciprocity that is an essential component of our relationship.

MF

Our relationship embodies a sentiment that was used to preface part II of the book: "You never know who will change you, or how." Because of this notion, of never knowing who can potentially change you for the better, my parents, Ali Farge and Aisha Mohamed, have always taught me the importance of putting your best foot forward in all encounters, including ours. And this coupled with your accessibility helped facilitate what I would describe as a rich relationship. Embracing the unknown as the authors point out invites us all to have a positive framework for building relationships.

While there are important intersections and resonances among the principles and standards between us, I see it as critical to emphasize and for readers to understand that our type of relationship is not exclusive to a duo that finds their values and priorities indistinguishable. In fact, this is precisely why we hear all too often of the importance of having different mentors for different aspects of life. The mentor you rely on for academic guidance may not be particularly capable of giving life guidance, and a life coach may not necessarily have the tools and resources needed to properly support during a turbulent time in your chosen career.

Understanding this notion is fundamental in finding and attracting mentors; once there is no stigma attached to having different mentors with different specializations, we begin to form the constellation of mentors the authors write about.

TE

I am reminded of the podcast that we did for Simon Fraser University's "Below the Radar" series as we conclude this afterword.[2] Do you have any reflections on that collaboration?

MF

Absolutely. Perhaps what I remember most was when we touched upon how, particularly at the time, the pandemic completely transformed and forced a reimagination as to what it meant to stay meaningfully connected. And it was during the height of the pandemic that the higher education enterprise saw many relationships falter due to the immense pressure that we were forced to reckon with. But also, the height of the pandemic did its part in re-emphasizing the importance of connectivity, and the extent to which it is important to value and nourish rich relationships.

We challenge readers of this book to seriously digest its stories. To go beyond the reading of these stories to actively pursue substantial relationships and to instigate perpetual cycles of mentorship.

Acknowledgments

WE OWE OUR GREATEST THANKS to the students we interviewed for this book (and for Peter and Leo's previous book as well), who shared stories and experiences with us about how much human relationships matter in college. Our student interviewees generously shared stories of vulnerability and struggle, as well as inspiration and joy, in hopes that their journeys might be valuable to other students. Their lessons represent the very heart and soul of this book, and we are grateful for the gifts of time and insight each person gave us.

Drew Koch, CEO of the John N. Gardner Institute for Excellence in Undergraduate Education, facilitated a grant to allow the electronic version of this book to be available free of charge, a tangible demonstration of JNGI's commitment to both excellence and equity.

We appreciate Timothy K. Eatman and Mohamed Farge's thoughtful afterword, and we thank them for sharing their wonderful partnership with our readers.

Many colleagues all over the globe gave us critical feedback on a draft manuscript, and their ideas shaped and refined our work immeasurably. We are grateful to US colleagues Karen Stout of Achieving the Dream; Bryce Bunting of Brigham Young University; Jeffrey Carpenter, Jon Dooley, Amaya Gaines, Jennie Goforth, Danielle Lake, and Maureen Vandermaas-Peeler of Elon University; Bryan Dewsbury of Florida International University; Leilani Carreño of Nevada State College; Joianne Smith of Oakton Community College; Sarah Hansen of the University of Iowa; Laura Rendón of the University of Texas at San Antonio; James Bridgeforth of Virginia Tech; and the children of two of our author team members, Katie Felten, Timothy Felten, and Kamilah Vega. International colleagues Luke Millard, Abertay University (Scotland); David Hornsby, Carleton University (Canada); Marca Wolfensberger, Hanze University of Applied Sciences (Netherlands); Janira Mendes Borges, King's College London (United Kingdom); Chng Huang Hoon, National University of Singapore; and Kelly Matthews, University of Queensland (Australia) broadened our perspectives in helpful ways.

We also express our gratitude to helpful individuals who introduced us to many of our student interviewees: Katie Felten and Samuel Owusu of Davidson College; Sat Gavassa and Roneet Merkin of Florida International University; Leilani Carreño of Nevada State College; Dawn Forbes Murphy of North Carolina A&T State University; Joianne Smith of Oakton Community College; Oralia De los Reyes of San Antonio College; Andrew Beckett and Sarah Hansen of the University of Iowa; and Shelby Newport and Tracey Wacker of the University of Michigan–Flint.

Our close and valued colleagues at Elon University, Robin Plummer, Christina Wittstein, Chris Sulva, and Andrea Sheetz, provided instrumental assistance with interview scheduling and transcription and the complex tasks of project management. Sandra Fields gave us helpful editorial guidance, and Carolyn Nelson envisioned an attractive visual design of the text.

We have had the pleasure of working with Greg Britton and Adriahna Conway of Johns Hopkins University Press on two projects and are immensely grateful for their advocacy and encouragement. Heidi Fritschel improved our manuscript greatly with her expert copyediting.

Finally, we treasure the encouragement, support, and patience of loved ones in our daily lives: Sara Walker; Laurie Lambert; Sinuhe, Delilah, and Kamilah Vega; and Kimberly Romero.

PF, LML, IAV, and OMT

College Terms to Know

Advisor. A professional who provides information, guidance, and support to students, such as an academic advisor.

Capstone. A course or experience completed near the end of your time in college, designed to help students integrate learning over time, oftentimes involving a culminating project or portfolio.

Civic engagement. Participation in the community through volunteer work, service learning, and other activities intended to identify and address issues of public concern.

Community partners. People and organizations (often nonprofit) that host students for civic engagement and typically provide mentoring and meaningful work experience, oftentimes linked to an academic class.

Counselor. A professional who helps students identify personal and academic goals, develop their strengths, and find potential solutions to problems.

Curriculum. The set of academic courses that make up the degree programs an institution is authorized to offer.

Dean. A senior academic leader, usually responsible for a school or division within the college or university.

Engaged learning. An educational approach that emphasizes active student participation in the learning experience both in and out of academic courses.

Faculty member. A professional whose responsibilities typically include teaching, research, and service to the institution; also sometimes known as a professor, instructor, or lecturer.

Finals. Exams, essays, and projects that students complete at the end of an academic term (such as an end-of-semester exam).

Food security. The measure of an individual's ability to consistently access food that is nutritious and sufficient in quantity.

Grade point average (GPA). A summary measure of academic performance based on a student's grades, often on a scale from 4.0 (A) to 0.0 (F).

Greek life. A common term for the activities of fraternities and sororities, which are student organizations principally organized around social and philanthropic activities.

Historically Black Colleges and Universities (HBCUs). Colleges or universities that were originally founded to educate students of African American descent.

Honors student. A student who is a member of an academic or other honors program.

Internship. Practical experience gained in a work setting, sometimes for academic credit or pay, and oftentimes linked to a student's academic program, such as an accounting internship.

Learning assistant. A student trained to facilitate learning by others students in a specific course or in an out-of-class setting (like a tutoring or writing center).

Learning community. A small group of students who share academic interests and who work together on organized activities; living-learning communities are programs that combine academic experiences with a residential living environment.

LinkedIn. The world's largest professional network on the internet to connect with colleagues and professional opportunities such as internships and jobs.

Major. The required and elective courses in a particular subject area that students specialize in while earning their degree.

Minor. A more limited (than in a major) set of required and elective courses in a particular subject area that students might choose to specialize in while earning their degree.

Office hours. Hours set by a faculty member to be available to meet with students to discuss coursework, academic interests, or other issues.

Orientation. A period, usually before the start of an academic term, when a variety of events are held to help new students transition to college.

Peer. A student.

Peer educator. A student trained facilitating learning by their peers (such as a learning assistant); this term is most often used to describe roles focused on students' personal development.

Pre-med student. A student taking classes designed to satisfy all the requirements needed for advanced education in medicine or health care.

Prerequisite. Something required as a prior condition for something else to happen or exist; for example, an introductory course (such as Psychology 101) is sometimes a prerequisite for enrolling in an upper-level course in a field (such as Psychology 201).

Professor. *See* Faculty member.

Provost. The chief academic officer of the college or university.

Residence hall. An on-campus facility owned by a college or university where students live.

Resident assistant or advisor (RA). A student leader who helps create a supportive and safe environment for students living in residence halls and other student housing.

Scholar. A person who has specialized expertise in a particular discipline or field and often has published books or articles in peer-reviewed journals.

Scholarship. Financial support awarded to a student based on academic achievement, financial need, a special talent (such as music or athletics), or other criteria.

Semester. An academic term of approximately fifteen weeks; there are generally two semesters (fall and spring) per academic year.

Service learning. An educational approach that connects academic learning with community service to both enrich learning and strengthen communities.

Staff member. An employee of a college or university supporting students or the institution in non-teaching areas such as student life, technology, facilities, and dining.

Student advisory board. A group of students who meet regularly to advise and guide a program or organization.

Student government association (SGA). An organization composed of elected students who represent the entire student body.

Study abroad/study away. An opportunity to pursue an educational program either internationally or domestically.

Summer bridge program. A program designed to ease the transition to college and support student success by providing students with academic skills and social resources needed to succeed in college; usually takes place in the summer or before college begins.

Supplemental instructor. *See* Learning assistant.

Syllabus. A written outline of the topics, readings, assignments, policies, and other important information related to a course, usually given to students (or posted online) at the start of the course.

Teaching assistant. A graduate student (sometimes an undergraduate student) who assists a faculty member with course responsibilities, such as leading small group discussions, grading, and providing one-on-one assistance to students.

Trustees. A governing group that determines an institution's policies and finances (including tuition), evaluates the president or chancellor, and advocates on behalf of the institution.

Tutor. Someone trained to provide individualized instruction to students outside of class.

Undergraduate research. A project conducted by an undergraduate student, with the support of a faculty mentor, that is designed to make an original intellectual or creative contribution to a discipline.

Withdrawal. A withdrawal occurs when an enrolled student acts to officially unenroll from one or more classes, typically early in the semester.

Work study. An on-campus job (often funded by the federal government) that provides part-time employment to students with financial need, allowing them to earn money while attending college.

Notes

INTRODUCTION

1. Matthew J. Mayhew et al., *How College Affects Students: 21st Century Evidence That Higher Education Works*, vol. 1 (San Francisco: Jossey-Bass, 2016).

2. Janice M. McCabe, *Connecting in College: How Friendship Networks Matter for Academic and Social Success* (Chicago: University of Chicago Press, 2016).

3. Lillian T. Eby, Tammy D. Allen, Sarah C. Evans, Thomas Ng, and David L. DuBois, "Does Mentoring Matter? A Multidisciplinary Meta-analysis Comparing Mentored and Non-mentored Individuals," *Journal of Vocational Behavior* 72, no. 2 (2008): 254–267; see also National Association of Colleges and Employers, "What Is Career Readiness?" (2021), https://www.naceweb.org/career-readiness/competencies/career-readiness-defined/.

4. For example, Peter Felten and Leo M. Lambert, *Relationship-Rich Education: How Human Connections Drive Success in College* (Baltimore: Johns Hopkins University Press, 2020).

5. Annie Murphy Paul, *The Extended Mind: The Power of Thinking outside the Brain* (Boston: Houghton Mifflin Harcourt, 2021), 192.

CHAPTER 1. START WITH ONE

1. Gallup and Purdue University, *Great Jobs, Great Lives: The 2014 Gallup-Purdue Index Report* (Washington, DC: Gallup; Lafayette, IN: Purdue University, 2014), 4, https://www.gallup.com/file/services/176768/GallupPurdueIndex_Report_2014.pdf.

2. Leo M. Lambert, Jason Husser, and Peter Felten, "Mentors Play Critical Role in Quality of College Experience, New Poll Suggests," *The Conversation*, August 22,

2018, https://theconversation.com/mentors-play-critical-role-in-quality-of-college-experience-new-poll-suggests-101861.

3. Saundra McGuire, *Teach Yourself How to Learn: Strategies You Can Use to Ace Any Course at Any Level* (Sterling, VA: Stylus, 2018).

CHAPTER 2. COLLEGE COMES WITH CHALLENGES

1. Xueli Wang, *On My Own: The Challenge and Promise of Buidling Equitable STEM Transfer Pathways* (Cambridge, MA: Harvard Education Press, 2020).

2. L. A. Schreiner, M. C. Louis, and D. D. Nelson, eds., *Thriving in Transitions: A Research-Based Approach to College Student Success* (Columbia, SC: University of South Carolina National Research Center for the First-Year Experience and Students in Transition, 2012).

3. Anna Parkman, "The Imposter Phenomenon in Higher Education: Incidence and Impact," *Journal of Higher Education Theory and Practice* 16, no. 1 (February 2016): 51–60; Rebecca D. Cox, *The College Fear Factor: How Students and Professors Misunderstand One Another* (Cambridge, MA: Harvard University Press, 2009).

4. Blake R. Silver, *The Cost of Inclusion: How Student Conformity Leads to Inequality on College Campuses* (Chicago: University of Chicago Press, 2020).

5. Saundra Yancy McGuire, *Teach Yourself How to Learn: Strategies You Can Use to Ace Any Course at Any Level* (Sterling, VA: Stylus, 2018).

6. Silver, *The Cost of Inclusion*.

7. Stephen John Quaye, Shaun R. Harper, and Samun L. Pendukar, eds., *Student Engagement in Higher Education: Theoretical Perspectives and Practical Approaches for Diverse Populations*, 3rd ed. (New York: Routledge, 2020).

8. Annemarie Vaccaro and Barbara M. Newman, "Development of a Sense of Belonging for Privileged and Minoritized Students: Am Emergent Model," *Journal of College Student Development* 57, no. 8 (November 2016): 925–942, http://doi.org/10.1353/csd.2016.0091.

9. Anthony Abraham Jack, *The Privileged Poor: How Elite Colleges Are Failing Disadvantaged Students* (Cambridge, MA: Harvard University Press, 2020).

CHAPTER 3. YOU HAVE WHAT IT TAKES

1. Tara J. Yosso, "Whose Culture Has Capital? A Critical Race Theory Discussion of Community Cultural Wealth," *Race Ethnicity and Education* 8, no. 1 (March 1, 2005): 69–91, https://doi.org/10.1080/1361332052000341006.

2. Daniel J. Almeida, Andrew M. Byrne, Rachel M. Smith, and Saul Ruiz, "How Relevant Is Grit? The Importance of Social Capital in First-Generation College Students' Academic Success," *Journal of College Student Retention: Research, Theory and Practice* 23, no. 3 (2021): 539–559, https://doi.org/10.1177/1521025119854688.

3. Matthew J. Mayhew, Alyssa N. Rockenbach, Nicholas A. Bowman, Tricia A. Seifert, and Gregory C. Wolniak, *How College Affects Students: 21st Century Evidence That Higher Education Works* (San Francisco: Jossey-Bass, 2016), 38.

4. Richard Arum and Josipa Roksa, *Academically Adrift: Limited Learning on College Campuses* (Chicago: University of Chicago Press, 2011).

5. This exercise is adapted from adapted from Kathy Cox, "Tools for Building on Youth Strengths," *Reclaiming Children and Youth: The Journal of Strength-based Interventions* 16 (2008): 19–24.

CHAPTER 4. CONNECTING WITH PEERS

1. Matthew J. Mayhew et al., *How College Affects Students: 21st Century Evidence That Higher Education Works* (San Francisco: Jossey-Bass, 2016).

2. Leo M. Lambert, Jason Husser, and Peter Felten, "Mentors Play Critical Role in Quality of College Experience, New Poll Suggests," *The Conversation*, August 22, 2018, https://theconversation.com/mentors-play-critical-role-in-quality-of-college -experience-new-poll-suggests-101861.

3. Janice M. McCabe, *Connecting in College: How Friendship Networks Matter for Academic and Social Success* (Chicago: University of Chicago Press, 2016).

CHAPTER 5. CONNECTING WITH PROFESSORS

1. Matthew J. Mayhew et al., *How College Affects Students: 21st Century Evidence That Higher Education Works* (San Francisco: Jossey-Bass, 2016).

2. Leo Lambert, Jason Husser, Peter and Felten, "Mentors Play Critical Role in Quality of College Experience, New Poll Suggests," *The Conversation*, August 22, 2018, https://theconversation.com/mentors-play-critical-role-in-quality-of-college -experience-new-poll-suggests-101861.

3. Ken Bain, *What the Best College Teachers Do* (Cambridge, MA: Harvard University Press, 2004); Tracie Marcella Addy, Derek Dube, Khadijah A. Mitchell, and Mallory SoRelle, *What Inclusive Instructors Do: Principles and Practices for Excellence in College Teaching* (Sterling, VA: Stylus, 2021).

4. Elisabeth Barnett, "Faculty Leadership and Student Persistence: A Story from Oakton Community College," *The Mixed Methods Blog* (Community College Research Center, Teachers College, Columbia University), May 9, 2018, https://ccrc .tc.columbia.edu/blog/faculty-leadership-student-persistence-oakton-community -college.html.

CHAPTER 6. CONNECTING WITH STAFF

1. Terrell L. Strayhorn, "Reframing Academic Advising for Student Success: From Advisor to Cultural Navigator," *NACADA Journal* 35, no. 1 (2015): 56–63.

2. Gary R. Pike, George D. Kuh, and Ryan C. Massa-McKinley, "First-Year Students' Employment, Engagement, and Academic Achievement: Untangling the Relationship between Work and Grades," *Journal of Student Affairs Research and Practice* 45, no. 4 (2008): 1012–34, https://doi.org/10.2202/1949-6605.2011.

3. George S. McClellan, Kristina L. Creager, and Marianna Savoca. *A Good Job: Campus Employment as a High-Impact Practice* (Sterling, VA: Stylus, 2018).

CHAPTER 7. RELATIONSHIP ACCELERATORS

1. Marta Zaraska, *Growing Young: How Friendship, Optimism, and Kindness Can Help You Live to 100* (New York: Penguin Random House, 2020).

2. Jessie L. Moore, "Key Practices for Fostering Engaged Learning," *Change: The Magazine of Higher Learning* 53, no. 6 (November 2, 2021): 12–18, https://doi.org/10.1080/00091383.2021.1987787.

3. Ashley Finley and Tia McNair, *Assessing Underserved Students' Engagement in High-Impact Practices* (Washington, DC: Association of American Colleges and Universities, 2013).

4. George Kuh, Ken O'Donnell, and Carol Geary Schneider, "HIPs at Ten," *Change: The Magazine of Higher Learning* 49, no. 5 (September 3, 2017): 8–16, https://doi.org/10.1080/00091383.2017.1366805.

CHAPTER 8. MAKE THE MOST OF MENTORING CONVERSATIONS

1. Terrell L. Strayhorn, *College Students' Sense of Belonging: A Key to Educational Success for All Students*, 1st ed. (New York: Routledge, 2012); Darnell Cole, Christopher B. Newman, and Liane I. Hypolite, "Sense of Belonging and Mattering among Two Cohorts of First-Year Students Participating in a Comprehensive College Transition Program," *American Behavioral Scientist* 64, no. 3 (March 1, 2020): 276–97, https://doi.org/10.1177/0002764219869417.

2. Laura I. Rendón, "Validating Culturally Diverse Students: Toward a New Model of Learning and Student Development," *Innovative Higher Education* 19, no. 1 (September 1994): 33–51, https://doi.org/10.1007/BF01191156.

CHAPTER 9. BUILDING YOUR RELATIONSHIP CONSTELLATION

1. W. Brad Johnson, *On Being a Mentor: A Guide for Higher Education Faculty*, 2nd ed. (New York: Routledge, 2016).

2. Janice McCabe, *Connecting in College: How Friendship Networks Matter for Academic and Social Success* (Chicago: University of Chicago Press, 2016).

3. Priscilla Claman, "Forget Mentors: Employ a Personal Board of Directors," *Harvard Business Review* (October 20, 2010), https://hbr.org/2010/10/forget-mentors-employ-a-person.

AFTERWORD

1. Peter Felten and Leo M. Lambert, *Relationship-Rich Education: How Human Connections Drive Success in College* (Baltimore: Johns Hopkins University Press, 2020).

2. Timothy Eatman and Mohamed Farge, "Community-Engaged Learning," May 18, 2021, in *Below the Radar*, hosted by Am Johal, podcast, Simon Fraser University, https://www.sfu.ca/vancity-office-community-engagement/below-the-radar -podcast/episodes/121-timothy-eatman-mohamed-farge.html.

Index